OREGON & WASHINGTON PERSONAL LINES LAW SUMMARY

SMITH FREED & EBERHARD P.C.
Your Litigation Partner

OREGON & WASHINGTON PERSONAL LINES LAW SUMMARY

Table of Contents- Oregon

Table of Contents- Washington

OREGON
PERSONAL LINES

I.   OREGON PROCEDURE

A.   STATUTE OF LIMITATIONS

Oregon statutes of limitations vary depending upon the claims asserted.

Action	Time Limitation	Source
Claims Against the Government	Action must be commenced within 2 years after the loss or injury. Notice of a claim must be provided to the Public entity within 180 days, regardless of the claimant's age. Notice requirement is extended to 1 year when the injury is death.	ORS 30.275(2) and (9)
Contracts	6 years; may be subject to a discovery rule.	ORS 12.080
Construction, Alteration or Repair to Real Property	10 years from the date of substantial completion.	ORS 12.135(1)
Contribution	2 years after settlement or judgment.	ORS 31.810
Defamation (libel/slander)	1 year.	ORS 12.120(2)
Indemnity	6 years after the date of payment.	ORS 12.080; *Huff v. Shiomi*, 73 Or App 605, 699 P2d 1178 (1985).
Landlord/ Tenant Actions	1 year for actions brought under Oregon's Residential Landlord Tenant Act. Common law actions (e.g., negligence, contract and trespass) remain the same.	ORS 12.125; ORS 90.100-90.840
Land/Real Property (including trespass)	6 years.	ORS 12.080(3)
Personal Injury (i.e., negligence, assault, battery, etc.)	2 years from discovery of injury. Any action must be commenced within 10 years of negligent act or omission.	ORS 12.110; ORS 12.115(1)
Personal Property (car)	6 years.	ORS 12.080(4)
Product Liability	2 years from when the plaintiff discovered that a product caused injury. Generally, the injury must have occurred within 10 years from the date that the product was first	ORS 30.905; ORS 30.907; ORS 30.908

	purchased for use or consumption.	
Survival of Actions (claimant dies before an action can be brought)	Personal representative must bring the action within 1 year of the individual's death.	ORS 12.190(1)
Wrongful Death	3 years from the death-causing injury.	ORS 30.020(1)

B. TOLLING (EXTENDING) THE STATUTE OF LIMITATIONS

1. Minor Claimants and Claimants with Personal Disabilities

If the claimant is under the age of 18 or insane, the time for bringing the claim is suspended for the period of minority or insanity. See ORS 12.160. But, the time for bringing the action cannot be extended for more than 5 years, or more than 1 year after the person attains 18 years of age, or more than 1 year after the person is no longer insane. ORS 12.160.

Note: The statute of limitations is also tolled for an action for the recovery of medical expenses incurred by a parent or guardian on behalf of a child for the same period of time as the child's claim, as long as the medical expenses resulted from the same events as the child's cause of action. ORS 12.160.

2. Advance Payment by Insurer

The statute of limitations tolls if advanced payments are made on either bodily injury or property damage, and the statutorily required notice letter is not sent within 30 days of the first payment. See Proposed Forms, Appendix 1. ORS 12.155; Blanton v. Beiswenger, 195 Or App 335, 97 P3d 1247 (2004).

    a.   ORS 12.155 does not apply exclusively to insurance companies. For the purposes of tolling the statute of limitations, the statute can apply to any "person" as defined by ORS 174.100(5) who makes an advanced payment (including individuals, corporations, associations, firms, partnerships, LLCs and joint stock companies). *Hamilton v. Paynter*, 342 Or 48, 149 P3d 131 (2006).

    b.   If an insurer makes an advanced payment to the co-owner of a vehicle that sustains damages, a notice of the statute of limitations must be provided to each co-owner, not just the owner that received the advance payment. ORS 12.155; *Snyder v. Espino-Brown*, 350 Or 141, 252 P3d 318 (2011).

c.   Medical expense payments which are required regardless of fault do not constitute advanced payments for purposes of tolling the statute of limitations. *Meoli v. Brown*, 200 Or App 44, 114 P3d 507 (2005).

3.   Death of Claimant's Attorney

The statute of limitations tolls for up to 180 days when a party's attorney dies before filing the action. The attorney must have agreed to represent the person in the action, the attorney-client relationship must have been reduced to writing by the attorney, and the action must have still been timely on the day of the attorney's death. ORS 12.195.

4.   Military Service

The period of a service-member's military service may not be included in computing time limits for statute of limitations purposes. This provision applies to actions filed in both federal and state court. ORS 399.238 (5).

C.   COMMENCEMENT OF THE ACTION

1.   An action is commenced when the complaint is filed. ORCP 3; ORS 12.020

2.   For the purpose of statute of limitations, the plaintiff has 60 days from the date of filing the complaint to perfect service. ORCP 7.

D.   SERVICE METHODS

1.   Personal Service

Hand delivery of a copy of the complaint to the person named as the defendant. ORCP 7(D)(2)(a).

2.   Substituted Service

a.   Delivery of the summons and complaint to residence with any resident who is 14 years of age or older; and

b.   Send true copies of the summons and complaint by first-class mail to the defendant's residence, business, or usual place of abode, together with a statement of the date, time and place at which substituted service was made. ORCP 7(D)(2)(b).

3.   Office Service

a.   Deliver a copy of the summons and the complaint to the office during normal working hours and leave with the person who is apparently in charge; and

b. Send the summons and complaint by first-class mail to the defendant's residence, business, or place most reasonably calculated to apprise defendant of the action, together with a statement of the date, time and place at which the office service was made. ORCP 7(D)(2)(c).

4. Service by Mail

When required or allowed by a rule or statute-

a. Send summons and complaint by certified, registered or first-class mail.

b. Computation of time for the completion of service:

  i. The day defendant signs a receipt for the mailing; or

  ii. 3 days after the mailing (if mailed within the state); or

  iii. 7 days if mailed outside the state. ORCP 7(D)(2)(d).

5. Service for Actions Arising Out of the Use of the Roadways

a. In any action arising out of any accident, collision, or other event giving rise to liability in which a motor vehicle may be involved while being operated upon the roadways, so long as the plaintiff makes at least one attempt to serve a defendant who operated such motor vehicle by the primary service methods (personal, office and substitute), the plaintiff may serve the defendant through certified mail to all of the following addresses:

  i. Residence address provided by the defendant at the scene of the accident;

  ii. Any residence address listed with the Department of Transportation; and

  iii. Any other address known to the plaintiff reasonably calculated to apprise defendant of the action.

b. Sufficient service pursuant to this subparagraph may be shown if the proof of service includes a true copy of the envelope in which each of the certified, registered, or express mailings was made showing that it was returned to sender as undeliverable or that the defendant did not sign the receipt.

c.   For the purpose of computing any period of time prescribed or allowed by these rules, service under this subparagraph shall be complete on the latest date on which any of the mailings required by (a), (b), and (c) above is made.

d.   If the mailing required by (c) is omitted because the plaintiff did not know of any address other than those specified in (a) and (b) above, the proof of service shall so certify. ORCP 7(D)(4)(a)(i).

E.   APPEARANCE BY THE DEFENDANT

1.   Defendant has 30 days from the time of service to file a response with the court. ORCP 7(C)(2).

2.   If plaintiff is notified in writing that a party intends to appear, plaintiff must give at least 10 days notice before filing for a default judgment. ORCP 69(A)(1).

3.   Oregon courts will not allow claims to sit, regardless of consent by plaintiff's counsel. Oregon courts may, on their own motion, dismiss a claim if no answer is filed. ORCP 69(B).

F.   COURT SYSTEMS IN OREGON

1.   Small Claims

a.   **Jurisdiction:**

i.   Mandatory jurisdiction for claims up to $750.

ii.   Optional jurisdiction for claims up to $10,000. ORS 46.405.

b.   **Service**: The claim may be served on the defendant either in the manner described above, or by certified mail. Defendant must respond within 14 days. ORS 46.445.

c.   **No lawyers** are allowed in small claims without express permission from the judge of the court. ORS 46.415(4).

i.   If, however, the party is a corporation, where an attorney must represent the corporation, a judge will likely allow the attorney to represent the corporation in a small claims court.

d.   **Hearings** in small claims court are before a judge. If the defendant removes the case from small claims court by demanding a jury trial or counter-sues for an amount exceeding $10,000 and does not prevail, the court shall give plaintiff reasonable attorney fees up to $1,000. ORS 46.465(4)(a).

    i.   However, the Oregon Constitution provides a right to trial by jury for any amounts in controversy over $750.

e.   **Duty to defend** can be fulfilled if counsel assists the insured in small claims, or removes the case to Circuit Court.

2.   Circuit Court

a.   *One-year rule: Oregon courts typically require that a case be concluded by its one-year anniversary.*

b.   **Discovery practices – "Trial by ambush":**

    i.   No discovery of expert witnesses.

    ii.   No interrogatories.

    iii.   "Body-part rule" – Discovery of medical records are limited to the body part at issue in personal injury cases.

c.   **Pleadings:**

    i.   Oregon requires fact pleadings. The pleader must allege facts that, if proved, will establish a right to relief. ORCP 18.

    ii.   Oregon rules do not require defendants to bring their counter claims (i.e. no compulsory counterclaims). However, a party pursuing a claim for damages must bring all claims arising out of the action or occurrence at one time. ORCP 22.

G.   ADR – COURT MANDATED ARBITRATION

1.   Generally, each court is required to establish mandatory arbitration for civil matters involving $50,000 or less. ORS 36.400.

2.   Either party may choose to appeal the result of the arbitration to a jury trial.

a.   If the defendant requests *trial de novo* but the position of the defendant does not improve, the defendant must pay the plaintiff's attorney fees up to 20% of the judgment. ORS 36.425(5)(a).

    b.   If the plaintiff requests *trial de novo* but the position of the plaintiff is not improved, plaintiff must pay defendant's attorney fees up to 10% of the amount claimed in the complaint. ORS 36.425(5)(b).

II.   OREGON BASICS OF LIABILITY AND TORT

A.   MOTOR VEHICLE AND PEDESTRIAN DUTIES

1.   Auto

    a.   **Basic Rule**: A driver must not drive at a speed greater than is reasonable and prudent under the circumstances. ORS 811.100.

    b.   **Oregon's Vehicle Code Prescribes the Duties of a Driver**: If a driver fails to comply with a statutory duty, the violation may be used to establish statutory negligence, or "negligence per se." (Exceptions in some circumstances if conduct is "reasonable.") Gattman v. Favro, 306 Or 11, 757 P2d 402 (1988).

    c.   **Traffic Citations** are not evidence of negligence. ORS 41.905.

    d.   **Seatbelt Defense**: Failure of the claimant to wear a seatbelt mitigates damages up to 5%. ORS 31.760.

2.   Auto v. Pedestrian

    a.   Vehicle drivers must stop and remain stopped for pedestrians if:

        i.   A pedestrian is within a marked or unmarked crosswalk. ORS 811.028; ORS 801.220; or

        ii.   In any of the following locations:

            1)   In the lane in which the driver's vehicle is traveling;

            2)   In a lane adjacent to the lane in which the driver's vehicle is traveling;

            3)   In the lane into which the driver's vehicle is turning;

4) In a lane adjacent to the lane into which the driver's vehicle is turning, if the driver is making a turn at an intersection that does not have a traffic control device under which a pedestrian may proceed as provided under ORS 814.010; or

5) Less than six feet from the lane into which the driver's vehicle is turning, if the driver is making a turn at an intersection that has a traffic control device under which a pedestrian may proceed as provided under ORS 814.010. ORS 811.028.

iii. A pedestrian is traveling on a sidewalk. ORS 811.025; or

iv. A pedestrian is proceeding in accordance with pedestrian control signals or in accordance with any traffic control device. ORS 811.028.

b. Pedestrians must yield to vehicles and may not:

i. Suddenly leave a curb or other place of safety and move into the path of a vehicle that is so close as to constitute an immediate hazard; or

ii. Cross a roadway at any point other than within a marked crosswalk or unmarked crosswalk at an intersection. ORS 814.040.

3. **Auto v. Animal**

a. The driver of a vehicle must:

i. Yield to the right of way to livestock being driven on a highway;

ii. Use caution when approaching or passing a person riding, leading, or herding livestock; and

iii. Stop if a person riding or leading livestock upon a highway gives a distress signal. If requested, a driver must turn off the engine until the livestock is controlled. ORS 811.510.

b. An owner may be liable for allowing livestock to run at large in a "closed range" area or within certain designated highways. ORS 607.044; ORS 607.505-527.

c. An owner of livestock may not be liable for allowing livestock to run in "open range" areas. *Piper v. Scott*, 164 Or App 1, 988 P2d 919 (1999).

4. Motorcycles and Bicycles

a. Bicyclists under the age of 16, motorcyclists, their passengers, and moped drivers must wear protective headgear. ORS 814.260; ORS 814.269; ORS 814.275; ORS 814.489; and ORS 814.485(1).

b. Failure of a bicyclist to wear a helmet is inadmissible to reduce damages or constitute a defense in an action for the bicyclist's damages. ORS 814.489.

c. Failure of a moped or motorcycle operator to wear a helmet may be used as evidence to reduce damages (because no statute provides otherwise.)

d. Insurers who write motorcycle policies are required to give a rate discount if the insured completed a state-organized motorcycle rider education course no more than 3 years prior to seeking insurance.

   i. Only one discount per motorcycle per operator (i.e., if the insured rider owns 3 motorcycles, the discount only applies to one motorcycle, not all three).

e. If the policy provides coverage for a motorcycle and other vehicles, the discount is only to the motorcycle share of the premium.

f. This law is not applicable to motorcycles used for business.

B. CLAIMS BETWEEN FAMILY MEMBERS & AGAINST CHILDREN

1. Familial Immunity

a. Spousal immunity is no longer available to bar a negligence action between spouses. *Heino v. Harper*, 306 Or 347, 759 P2d 253 (1988).

b. Parents are not immune from personal torts, such as negligence, when operating a motor vehicle. Parents are immune from torts arising out of their parental relationship, unless the parent acted wantonly and willfully. *Winn v. Gilroy*, 296 Or 718, 681 P2d 776 (1984).

i.   Minors are held to the standard of a reasonable person of like age, intelligence, and experience under similar circumstances. *Thomas v. Inman*, 282 Or 279, 578 P2d 399 (1978).

ii.   Custodial parents are responsible for the intentional or reckless acts of their unemancipated minor children up to $7,500. ORS 30.765.

C.   NEGLIGENCE CLAIMS

1.   Generally

Absent a "special relationship," negligence occurs when the defendant's conduct unreasonably created a foreseeable risk of harm of the kind that befell the plaintiff. *Fazzolari v. Portland School Dist. No. 1J,* 303 Or 1, 734 P2d 1326 (1987). What is deemed "reasonably foreseeable" for the purposes of establishing liability is quite broad and may, for example, even extend to negligent vehicle maintenance by a prior owner. *Bailey v. Lewis Farm, Inc.*, 343 Or 276, 171 P3d 336 (2007).

Note: A claim of negligence must be based on an actual, present harm or injury suffered by the plaintiff. Allegations that defendant's negligence merely increased plaintiff's risk of future harm is insufficient. Lowe v. Philip Morris USA, Inc., 207 Or App 532, 142 P3d 1079 (2006).

2.   Negligent Infliction of Emotional Distress

As a general rule, a plaintiff cannot recover for negligent infliction of emotional distress unless that person is physically injured, threatened with physical injury, or physically impacted by the tortious conduct. *See Lockett v. Hill*, 182 Or App 377, 380, 51 P3d 5 (2002); *Onita Pacific Corp. v. Trustees of Bronson,* 315 Or 149, 843 P2d 890 (1992).

Exception: Defendant's conduct infringes on some legally protected interest apart from causing the distress. See Lockett v. Hill, 182 Or App 377, 380, 51 P3d 5 (2002).

3.   Liability of a Vehicle Owner:

Permissive use of a vehicle does not automatically impute liability on the owner, unless one of the following applies:

a.   **Family Purpose Doctrine**: An owner who maintains an automobile for the pleasure or convenience of the owner's family is liable if a member of the family negligently uses the car for pleasure or convenience with the knowledge and consent of the owner. *Kraxberger v. Rogers*, 231 Or 440, 373 P2d 647 (1962).

b.   **Negligent Entrustment**: Absent a special relationship between the parties, the claimant must allege that the other's entrustment was unreasonable under the circumstances, that it caused harm to the claimant, and that the risk of harm was foreseeable. *Matthews v. Federal Service Ins. Co.,* 122 Or App 124, 857 P2d 852 (1993).

    c.   **Agency or Joint Enterprise** exists, such as an employment relationship.

Note: Permissive use alone will <u>not</u> create liability.

D.   OREGON RESIDENTIAL LANDLORD TENANT ACT (ORLTA)

1.   Generally

ORLTA adds to the common-law rules that underlie premise liability in the landlord-tenant relationship. It creates a duty for the landlord to maintain the dwelling unit in a habitable condition. ORS 90.320.

2.   Habitability

A dwelling unit shall be considered uninhabitable if it substantially lacks:

    a.   Effective waterproofing and weather protection of roof and exterior walls;

    b.   Plumbing facilities maintained in good working order;

    c.   A water supply approved under applicable law;

    d.   Adequate heating facilities maintained in good working order;

    e.   Electrical lighting with wiring maintained in good working order;

    f.   Buildings, grounds and appurtenances at the time of the commencement of the rental agreement in every part safe for normal and reasonably foreseeable uses, clean, sanitary and free from all accumulations of debris, filth, rubbish, garbage, rodents and vermin, and all areas under control of the landlord kept in every part safe for normal and reasonably foreseeable uses, clean, sanitary and free from all accumulations of debris, filth, rubbish, garbage, rodents and vermin;

    g.   Appropriate receptacles for garbage that are regularly and properly emptied (unless the landlord-tenant agreement says otherwise);

    h.   Floors, walls, ceilings, stairways and railings maintained in good repair;

i. Ventilating, air conditioning and other facilities and appliances,

j. including elevators, maintained in good repair if supplied or required to be supplied by the landlord;

k. Safety from fire hazards, including a working smoke alarm; or

l. Working locks for all dwelling entrance doors. ORS 90.320.

3. Damages

a. Tenants may recover damages, including attorney fees and injunctive relief, which arise from the landlord's failure to maintain the dwelling in a habitable condition.

b. Tenants are not required to prove the landlord had actual or constructive knowledge of an uninhabitable condition to claim damages. *Davis v. Campbell,* 327 Or 584, 965 P2d 1017 (1998).

c. The tenant shall not be entitled to recover damages if the landlord neither knew nor should have known of the condition; and if:

 i. The tenant knew or reasonably should have known of the condition and failed to give actual notice to the landlord in a reasonable time prior to the occurrence of the personal injury, damage to personal property, diminution in rental value or other tenant loss resulting from the noncompliance; or

 ii. The condition was caused after the tenancy began by the deliberate or negligent act or omission of someone other than the landlord or a person acting on behalf of the landlord. ORS 90.360(2)(a)(b).

d. If neither the landlord nor the tenant knew or should have known of the uninhabitable condition, the landlord is likely to be held liable.

E. PREMISES LIABILITY

1. Invitee

a. An invitee is either a public invitee or a business invitee.

i.   A "business invitee" is defined as a person who is invited to enter or remain on the land for a purpose directly or indirectly connected with the business dealings with the possessor of the land. *Parker v. Hult Lumber & Plywood Co.*, 260 Or 1, 8, 488 P2d 454 (1971).

ii.   A "public invitee" is defined as a person who is invited to enter or remain on the land as a member of the public for the *purposes* to which the land is held open to the public. *Baker v. Lane County*, 28 Or App 53, 58, 588 P2d 1247 (1977).

b.   *Visitors who regularly provide beneficial services on residential property (i.e., package delivery persons) are, as a matter of law, invitees for the purposes of determining the level of duty a possessor of land owes them. Johnson v. Short, 213 Or App 255, 160 P3d 1004 (2007).*

c.   Invitees are owed the highest duty of care. As to an invitee, a possessor must:

i.   Exercise reasonable care to make the premises reasonably safe for an invitee (which may include the duty to inspect the premises); and

ii.   Warn of any danger that the invitee may not discover. *Woolston v. Wells*, 297 Or 548, 557-558, 687 P2d 144 (1984); *Hill v. Pacific Power & Light*, 273 Or 713, 715, 543 P2d 3 (1975); *Wilsey v. Campbell*, 255 Or 420, 467 P2d 964 (1970).

2. Licensee

a.   A licensee is a person who comes on to the premises for his or her own purpose with the consent of the possessor. *Rich v. Tite-Knot Pine Mill*, 245 Or 185, 191, 421 P2d 370 (1966). Thus, a licensee is any person who has a license, that is, a privilege to enter on the land.

b.   The consent of the possessor may be expressed or implied, and may be manifested by the possessor's actions as well as words. If the possessor's conduct gives a visitor reason to believe that he or she is privileged to enter, the visitor is a licensee. *Rich v. Tite-Knot Pine Mill*, 245 Or 185, 191, 421 P2d 370 (1966).

c. Social guests and public officers who enter the premises in the performance of their duties are considered licensees.

d. As to licensees, a possessor must warn of concealed dangers. *Bergman v. Cook,* 245 Or 163, 421 P2d 382 (1966).

3. Trespasser

a. A possessor of land is generally not liable for injuries caused by a trespasser unless:

   i. The possessor knows, or should know, that there are frequent trespassers. *Denton v. L.W. Vail Co. Inc.,* 23 Or App 28, 541 P2d 511 (1975);

   ii. The possessor engages in willful misconduct or reckless disregard for the safety of the trespasser. *Towe v. Sacagawea, Inc.,* 246 Or App 26, -- P---- (2011), review allowed, 246 Or App 26, 264 P.3d 184 (May 17,2012). It is important to note that this case is under review by the Oregon Supreme Court.

   iii. There is an attractive nuisance on the property that children, because of their youth, would not realize the danger of. *Baker v. Lane County,* 28 Or App 53, 588 P2d 1247 (1977).

F. DOG BITES

1. *No "One Bite Rule" for Economic Damages Claims*

Owner is strictly liable for economic damages caused by his or her dog (i.e. medical & hospital expenses, rehabilitative services, loss of income, past and future impairment of earning capacity, etc.). Furthermore, dog owners may not exercise the "lack of foreseeability" defense for claims seeking only economic damages, although other defenses, such as provocation of the dog, are specifically preserved by statute.

a. However, in order to establish a claim for non-economic damages, a plaintiff must prove that the attack could have been foreseen (*i.e.,* the dog had vicious tendencies.)

b. *The statute does not differentiate between personal injury and injury to property caused by the dog. ORS 31.360.*

2. Landlords

A landlord can be held liable for dog bites that occur away from the landlord's property if the landlord consents to such activity, or knows that it will be carried on the landlord's property and the landlord "knows or has reason to know that the activity will unavoidably involve an unreasonable risk of harm to persons off the rental property." *Park v. Hoffard*, 315 Or 624, 847 P2d 852 (1992).

G. TIMBER TRESPASS

1. Plaintiff will receive treble damages, plus costs and attorney fees, when there is a willful injury to trees, timber, produce, or shrubs on the plaintiff's land. ORS 105.810.

2. Plaintiff will receive double damages, plus costs and attorney fees, if damage was casual or involuntary, committed by the defendant who had probable cause to believe that the land belonged to the defendant; or if the removal was for the purpose of repairing a public highway or bridge. ORS 105.815(1).

3. Damages may include the cost of reforestation or the value of the trees up to the diminished value of the land. *Gerdes v. Bohemia*, 88 Or App 62, 68, 744 P2d 275 (1987).

H. LIQUOR LIABILITY

1. Liability to Others

Under the liquor liability statute, a licensee, permitee, or social host is liable for damages incurred by intoxicated patrons or guest only if:

a. *Alcoholic beverages were served while the patron or guest was visibly intoxicated; and*

b. *Plaintiff did not substantially contribute to the intoxication. ORS 471.565(2).*

Plaintiffs must prove the above two items by "clear and convincing" evidence. ORS 471.565(2).

2. Liability for Serving a Minor

No licensee, permitee or social host shall be liable to third persons injured by or through persons not having reached 21 years of age, unless a reasonable person would have:

a. Requested age identification; or

b. Determined that the identification was altered or did not accurately describe the person to whom the alcoholic liquor was sold or served. ORS 471.567.

In Oregon, a minor's parent or guardian may give, or otherwise make available, alcoholic liquor to the minor as long as the minor is in a private residence and is accompanied by the parent or guardian. ORS 471.410.

3. **Notice Requirement**

    a.   An action for damages caused by intoxicated patrons off the premises may be brought against a licensee, permitee or social host only if notice was given within the following timeline:

        i.   One year for damages arising out of wrongful death; or

        ii.   180 days for injuries other than wrongful death.

    b.   Notice requirement begins to accrue when the person asserting the claim discovers or reasonably should have discovered the existence of a claim.

    c.   Notice requirements do not apply to the following:

        i.   Claimants under 18 years of age or incapacitated;

        ii.   Claimants unable to give notice by reason of the injury or by reason of being financially incapable; or

        iii.   Claimants unable to determine identity of responsible party due to assertion of the server's right against self-incrimination.

    d.   Notice requirements are met under the following circumstances:

        i.   Formal notice is given in writing, asserting a claim for damages, describing the time, place and circumstances, and includes the claimant's name and address;

        ii.   Defendant had "actual notice" of the potential claim;

        iii.   An action is commenced by or on behalf of the claimant within the notice period. ORS 471.565.

I. STRICT LIABILITY

1. Oregon law applies strict liability for injuries resulting from "abnormally dangerous" or "ultra-hazardous" activities. In

determining whether an activity is "ultra-hazardous," the court will look at the potential for harm of an exceptional magnitude, probability for such harm despite the utmost care, and whether the activity is relatively common in the community. *Ellis v. Ferrell Gas*, 211 Or App 648, 156 P3d 136 (2007).

J. WRONGFUL DEATH AND SURVIVAL CLAIMS

1. A "wrongful death" action can be pursued by the personal representative of the estate for the benefit of the surviving spouse, children, stepchildren, parents and stepparents of the decedent. ORS 30.020.

2. Damages recoverable in wrongful death include:

    a. Reasonable charges for medical care and funeral expenses;

    b. Compensation for decedent's disability, pain and suffering;

    c. Pecuniary loss to decedent's estate;

    d. Pecuniary loss and compensation for loss of society, companionship, and services suffered by decedent's spouse, children and parents; and

    e. Punitive damages that the decedent would have been entitled to recover had he lived. ORS 30.020(2).

    f. "Noneconomic damages" in wrongful death are limited to $500,000 by statute. ORS 31.710; ORS 30.010-30.100.

3. A "survival" action is allowed for injury claims when the claimant's death is unrelated. Damages are limited. ORS 30.075.

4. Proper venue for wrongful death actions is the county where the negligence that caused the decedent's death occurred, not where the decedent died. *Howell v. Willamette Urology, P.C.*, 344 Or 124, 178 P3d 220 (2008).

K. SHARING THE FAULT

1. **Comparative Fault**

    a. *Plaintiff is barred from recovery if more than 50% at fault.*

    b. Defendant may not compare his or her fault to those immune from liability, those not subject to the court's jurisdiction, or those barred by a statute of limitations. ORS 31.600.

2.   **Joint and Several Liability**

> a.   *Defendants are severally, not jointly, liable for damages. The court shall determine the award of damages to each claimant in accordance with the percentages of fault determined by the trier of fact and shall enter judgment against each party determined to be liable. The court then shall enter a judgment in favor of the plaintiff against any third party defendant who is found to be liable in any degree, even if the plaintiff did not make a direct claim against the third party defendant. ORS 31.610(1)-(2).*

b.   However, upon motion made no later than one year after the judgment has become final, if the court determines that all or part of any party's share of the obligation is uncollectible the court will reallocate the uncollectible share among the other parties. ORS 31.610(3).

c.   But a party's share of the obligation cannot be increased if the claimant's percentage of fault is equal to or greater than the percentage of fault of the party, or the party's percentage is 25% or less. ORS 31.610(4).

L.   DAMAGES

1.   "Economic Damages"

Economic Damages means objectively verifiable monetary losses including, but not limited to, reasonable charges necessarily incurred for medical services, burial and memorial expenses, loss of income and past and future impairment of earning capacity, reasonable and necessary expenses incurred for substitute domestic services, damage to reputation that is economically verifiable, reasonable and necessarily incurred costs due to loss of use of property, and reasonable costs incurred for repair or replacement of damaged property, whichever is less. ORS 31.710.

a.   **Medical Write-offs**

Medical expenses written off by a medical provider pursuant to an agreement with the plaintiff's insurer are recoverable economic damages that may not be deducted from a post-jury verdict. Plaintiff is not precluded from receiving a double recovery. ORS 31.580. Rather, when a plaintiff receives an award for injuries from the injury-causing party as well as a third party, ORS 31.580 grants the trial court some discretion on reducing the plaintiff's judgment award by how much the plaintiff will receive from the third party (e.g. the insurer). However, the trial court's discretion is limited under ORS 31.580 if the third party benefits are federal Social Security benefits. A 2009 Oregon Supreme Court case, *White v. Jubitz*, held that Medicare benefits are federal Social Security benefits. 347 Or 212, 219 P3d 566 (2009). Thus, trial courts are prevented from reducing the jury award by the amount "written-off" under the Medicare benefits. *Id.* However, a defendant can submit evidence to prove that the amount of medical expenses claimed is excessive, and therefore unreasonable. *Id.*

2.   "Noneconomic Damages"

Noneconomic damages include subjective, nonmonetary losses including, but not limited to, pain, mental suffering, emotional distress, humiliation, injury to reputation, loss of care, comfort, companionship and society, loss of consortium, inconvenience and interference with normal and usual activities apart from gainful employment. ORS 31.710(2)(b).

> a.   *Noneconomic damages are not allowed for any plaintiff injured while driving:*
>
> i.   *Under the influence of intoxicants; or*
>
> ii.   *Without insurance, unless the driver was insured within 180 days of the accident and has not driven without insurance in the preceding year. ORS 31.715.*

Note: The Oregon Supreme Court upheld the constitutionality of this statute in Lawson v. Hoke, 339 Or 253, 119 P3d 210 (2005).

Exception: This limitation to noneconomic damages does not apply if the defendant was driving uninsured, driving under the influence of intoxicants, engaged in an intentional tort, driving reckless in violation of ORS 811.140 or engaged in felonious conduct. However, even if a plaintiff does not have insurance, a question of fact may exist as to whether a defendant was engaged in reckless driving sufficient to survive a motion for summary judgment to dismiss a plaintiff claims for non-economic damages. Morehouse v. Haynes,350 Or 318, 253 P3d 368 (2011).

b.   Noneconomic damages are unlimited, with two notable exceptions:

i.   In most wrongful death cases, noneconomic damages are limited to $500,000. ORS 31.710. *Hughes v. Peacehealth*, 204 Or App 614, 131 P3d 798 (2006).

ii.   Claims against public entities are subject to statutory limits. ORS 30.271; ORS 30.272; ORS 30.273.

Note: The statutory limit for noneconomic damages does not apply to bodily injury or property damage claims because it was held to be unconstitutional. Lankin v. Senco Products, Inc., 329 Or 62, 987 P2d 463 (1999).

c.   Noneconomic damages in the amount of $1 do not satisfy Oregon's general requirement that "some noneconomic damages" be awarded whenever economic damages in a negligence action are awarded. A jury may award economic damages without any accompanying noneconomic damages only if the following three things are true: (1) evidence of the plaintiff's injury is purely subjective; (2) the defendant presents evidence indicating that the plaintiff's injury is not caused by the accident; and (3) the objective evidence of a substantial injury is contradicted by other competent evidence or could be disbelieved by the jury. *Mays v. Vejo*, 224 Or App 426, 198 P3d 943 (2008). The Oregon Court of Appeals held in *Williams v. Funk* that plaintiffs that suffer substantial injuries, as opposed to only minor injuries, may have a jury instructed that any award of economic damages must be accompanied by an award of noneconomic damages. 230 Or App 142, 213 P3d 1275 (2009). However, the mere existence of an injury is not alone sufficient to necessitate a jury instruction that requires an award of noneconomic damages. *Id.*

3.   Punitive Damages

a.   Punitive damages are allowed if plaintiff proves by *clear and convincing* evidence that the defendant acted with:

   i.   malice or reckless and outrageous indifference to a highly unreasonable risk of harm; and

   ii.   a conscious indifference to the health safety and welfare of others. ORS 31.730(1).

b.   *There is a special procedure for asserting punitive damages. The claim cannot be asserted in the initial complaint. The party seeking punitive damages must give notice that they will seek punitive damages and then file a motion supported by evidence. The motion can be filed any time after the complaint is filed. ORS 31.725.*

c.   Punitive damages awards that punish a defendant for harm caused to people who are not parties to the litigation are unconstitutional. *Philip Morris USA v. Williams,* 549 US 346 (2007).

d. Although the United States Supreme Court determined that no bright-line rule regarding awards of punitive damages exists, the Court did hold that "few awards exceeding a single-digit ratio between punitive and compensatory damages…will satisfy due process." *State Farm Mut. Auto Ins. Co. v. Campbell*, 538 US 408 (2003). The Oregon Supreme Court held that generally punitive damages are constitutionally limited to 4 times economic damages where there is only an economic harm, as opposed to physical injury or risk to public health or safety and absent some particularly egregious circumstance. *Goddard v. Farmers Ins. Co.*, 344 Or 232, 179 P3d 645 (2008). However, if there are aggravating factors such as: the conduct was carried out with reckless disregard to the health or safety of others; the target of the conduct was financially vulnerable; the conduct was repeated; or the harm was the result of intentional malice, trickery or deceit, then the general rule may be set aside. *Hamlin v. Hampton Lumber Mills, Inc.*, 349 Or 526, 246 P3d 1121 (2011).

e. *The Oregon Supreme Court recently clarified that the state's 60% interest in punitive damages awards vests following the entry of the judgment, not the jury's verdict (therefore, the Court held the state's consent was not required before a settlement could be reached between the parties following the jury's verdict). Patton v. Target, 349 OR 230, 242 P3d 611 (2010); ORS 31.735.*

4. Attorney Fees

a. Fees are only recoverable when prescribed by statute or contract.

b. Claims Involving $10,000 or less - ORS 20.080

   i. *A plaintiff is allowed attorney fees if: (1) plaintiff files a claim for $10,000 or less on or after January 1, 2012 ($7,500 for claims filed between January 1, 2010 and December 31, 2011); (2) plaintiff makes a written demand on the defendant for payment, at least 30 days prior to filing an action; (3) plaintiff prevails on the claim and (4) plaintiff obtains a judgment for an amount greater than any pre-filing settlement offer made by defendant.*

ii.   Plaintiffs must provide medical records and bills, repair bills, estimates of repairs or a written estimate of the difference in value so that defendants and defendants' insurers are aware of the nature and scope of the claim.

iii.   The plaintiff's written demand must be made "in a manner reasonably calculated to apprise the defendant of the demand" at least 30 days before an action is filed. The written demand does not need to be sent by certified mail, or even to the insurance company handling the claim in order to meet this requirement. *Woods v. Carl Karcher Enterprises, Inc.*, 341 Or 549, 146 P3d 319 (2006).

iv.   A written demand must either: 1) identify a specific monetary amount or 2) reference the applicable statute (ORS 20.080) if a dollar amount is not specified in the written demand. Neither an oral demand by itself, nor an oral demand supplement to an incomplete written demand satisfies the statute's pre-filing requirement. *Johnson v. Swaim*, 343 Or 423, 172 P3d 645 (2007).

v.   A plaintiff may recover attorney fees under ORS 20.080 alleging multiple causes of action if it files a complaint seeking a total recovery of $10,000 or less so long as each individual cause of action seeks $10,000 or less. *Bedford v. Merety Monger Trust ex rel. Monger*, 251 Or. App. 778, --- P3d ----, (2012).

         For example, in Bedford v. Merety Monger Trust ex rel. Monger, 251 Or. App. 778, --- P3d ----, (2012), the Bedfords' shared a water delivery system with their neighbors who shut off the system depriving the Bedfords of their only water source. The Bedfords sought an implied easement and a nuisance. The damages pleaded for each theory of liability was less than the statutory maximum under ORS 20.080. Although the combined total damages award exceeded the maximum under ORS 20.080, the court concluded that since the claims were separate and distinct and the amount alleged in tort damages for each tort was below the statutory maximum, the Bedfords were entitled to attorney fees under ORS 20.080.

c. An offer of judgment will not reduce a plaintiff's ability to recover all of her attorney fees under ORS 20.080(1). If an ORS 20.080 claim is properly filed, there is no method to reduce or eliminate attorney fee exposure other than a pre-suit offer. *Powers v. Quigley,* 345 Or 432, 198 P3d 919 (2008).

d. Failure to settle claims within 6 months - ORS 742.061.

  i. An insurer can be liable for attorney fees awarded to the insured if the insurer failed to settle the claim within six months of receiving a "proof of loss" if the insured ultimately recovers more than the insurer's settlement offer.

Note: ORS 742.061 does not require a "proof of loss" be in writing; oral notice can be sufficient. Parks v. Farmers Ins. Co., 347 Or 374, 227 P3d 1127 (2009).

  ii. ORS 742.061 applies to all policies regardless of where the policy is issued or delivered so long as the case is filed in Oregon. *Morgan v. Amex Assurance Co.,* 352 Or. 363, 287 P3d 1038 (2012).

  iii. An insurer is not liable for attorney fees if it has accepted coverage and the only issues are the liability of the uninsured or underinsured motorist and the damages due the insured and the insurer has consented to submit the case to binding arbitration.

Note: The Oregon Court of Appeals recently held that despite sending a letter consenting to coverage, if an insurer denies one or more of a claimant's medical bills, the insurer has not actually consented to coverage under ORS 742.061 and therefore may be still liable for the claimant's attorney fees. Badrick v. Farmers, 238 Or App 320, 242 P3d 685 (2010).

M. **SETTLEMENT**

  1. **Settlement Between Two Parties**

A settlement is a contract subject to the basic rules of contract law. *Ristau v. Wescold, Inc.,* 318 Or 383, 868 P2d 1331 (1994). An oral settlement is valid only if it can be proven.

a.   Settlement With a Minor or Incapacitated Person

Minors are unable to enter into binding settlement agreements with persons against whom they have a claim.

i.   A person with legal custody of a minor may settle a claim on behalf of the minor without court approval, provided:

1)   The amount of the claim is $25,000 or less, not including reimbursement for medical expenses, liens, attorney fees, or costs of a lawsuit;

2)   The settlement funds are paid into a federally insured savings account in the sole name of the minor; and

3)   The parent/custodian attests that the minor will be fully compensated by the settlement or that there is no practical way to obtain additional funds. ORS 126.725

ii.   The signature of the child's legal custodian on a settlement agreement is binding on the minor and has the same force and effect as if the minor was a competent adult entering into the settlement his or herself.

iii.   A legal custodian is not liable to the minor for claims arising out of the settlement, so long as the custodian acts in good faith.

iv.   ORS 126.725 requires settlement awards to be deposited "solely in the name of the minor" and expressly enables minors to contract with banks to create this type of account.

1)   An attorney representing a minor must deposit the settlement award into a federally insured savings account. However, if the minor is unrepresented, the payor or defense attorney must deposit the funds. After the funds are deposited, notice must be given by personal service or by first-class mail to the minor.

2)   Minors cannot withdraw, remove, or transfer the settlement award unless the minor

obtains a court order, becomes 18 years old, or dies. ORS 126.725

v.   For claims larger than $25,000, parents do not have the authority to enter settlement agreements for their children. A conservator must be appointed by the court. ORS 126.725 (1)(b).

     b.   **Settlement with Plaintiff When Multiple Parties Are at Fault**

The covenant not to sue must be obtained in "good faith" in order to fully protect against claims made by plaintiff. The settlement with the plaintiff will protect the defendant from co-defendant, except for theories based on indemnity. ORS 31.815; *State By and Through State Acc. Ins. Fund Corp. v. Barkman*, 101 Or App 20, 789 P2d 8 (1990).

     c.   **Settlement of a Wrongful Death Claim**

The court must approve all settlements involving a deceased, except when the release is signed by the sole heirs. ORS 30.070; *Busch v. Farmington Centers of Beaverton*, 203 Or App 349, 124 P3d 1282 (2005).

     d.   **Third-Party Settlements**

Defendant settles the case with plaintiff and then seeks indemnity from a third-party. Indemnity is only proper if the settlement between the plaintiff and defendant included a release as to the plaintiff's claims against the third-party. *Moore Excavating, Inc. v. Consolidated Supply Co.,* 186 Or App 324, 63 P3d 592 (2003).

III.   OREGON BASICS OF AUTO INSURANCE LAW

A.   LIABILITY INSURANCE (THIRD PARTY)

1.   Financial Responsibility Law

     a.   Liability coverage must provide coverage for:

         i. $25,000 per person

         ii. $50,000 per accident

         iii. $20,000 property damage. ORS 806.070(2).

Note: The Oregon legislature recently amended ORS 806.070(2) by increasing the required minimum amount of acceptable property damage coverage from $10,000 to $20,000 for all policies issued or renewed on or after January 1, 2010. Any policies not issued or renewed on or after January 1, 2010 are still subject to the $10,000 property damage minimum liability coverage.

b. Uninsured/Underinsured Motorist protection must equal liability coverage limits unless a named insured elects to lower limits in writing. ORS 742.500(1).

c. Liability insurance policies must provide liability coverage for vehicles provided to the insured on a temporary basis while the insured's vehicle is being serviced or repaired. ORS 742.450(5).

d. An insurer may not require that an insured make the repairs to the insured's motor vehicle as a condition for recovery under a motor vehicle liability insurance policy. Insurers must inform consumers of this prohibition by (1) requiring express notification prior to giving a preferred repair shop recommendation and (2) written notice within three days of an insured's acceptance of a preferred shop recommendation. ORS 746.280.

e. **Self-Insured Companies**

Oregon's Financial Responsibility Law allows entities that own at least 25 vehicles to "self-insure" by promising to provide the same coverage as required by the FRL (at least $25,000 per person, $50,000 per accident). ORS 806.130.

i. Self-insurers (*e.g.,* rental car companies) must cover any permissive drivers of their vehicles with liability insurance up to the state minimum, though a self-insurer is not required to insure anyone who operates one of its vehicles without its permission.

ii. Any liability or uninsured motorist coverage from the self-insurer is secondary to coverage otherwise available to the customer of the self-insurer, an operator of the self-insured vehicle, or an occupant of the self-insured vehicle. Further, the self-insured coverage is a "disappearing coverage" (*i.e.,* if there exists 25/50 coverage elsewhere, the self-insurer has no coverage).

iii. The self-insurer may recover from the permissive driver of its vehicle any money it paid on the driver's behalf to an injured party.

iv. Injured parties may collect from their UM/UIM coverage if they are injured by a self-insured vehicle if the amount they recover from the self-insurer is less than the UM/UIM liability limit of their own policy. ORS 742.502(6).

f.   **Rental Car Companies**

A business that rents a vehicle in the course of its business is not liable for damage that arises out of the use of the vehicle by the person who rents the vehicle.

    i.   The limitation does not apply if the business providing the vehicle is negligent in maintaining or in providing the vehicle to the renter.

    ii.   To take advantage of the limitation on liability, the parties must agree in writing to the limitation. ORS 30.135.

2.   **Exclusions**

The Financial Responsibility Act voids many auto policy exclusions up to $25,000 per person, such as the intra-family exclusion or under-21 exclusion. ORS 742.450. All policies issued or renewed after January 1, 2008 may not contain "family member" or "household" exclusions. All Oregon motor vehicle liability insurance policies must provide liability coverage for family members residing in the same household as the insured in an amount equal to the amount of liability coverage purchased by the insured. ORS 742.450(8).

3.   **Duty to Defend**

a.   **8 Corner Rule**

Oregon law states that only the terms of the insurance policy and the allegations of the complaint can be considered when determining whether there is a duty to defend. Information that an insurer obtains during the course of its investigation cannot be considered when determining the duty to defend. *State Farm Fire & Cas. Co. v. Sevier*, 272 Or 278, 537 P2d 88 (1975).

Note: However, that a recent Oregon Court of Appeals case held that while applying the "eight-corners" rule makes sense in determining whether alleged conduct falls within the scope of coverage, there is no logical justification for limiting to the four-corners of the complaint a determination of a party's status as an insured (which the Court called a preliminary question to whether conduct is covered). Fred Shearer & Sons, Inc. v. Gemini, 237 Or App 468, 240 P3d 67 (2010).

b.   **Insurance Application**

An insurance application becomes part of the policy only when it is delivered to the insured with the policy. Progressive Ins. v. National Am. Ins. Co. of Cal., 201 Or App 301, 118 P3d 836 (2005).

c.   **Lesser Included Claims**

There is a duty to defend even when the claim alleged in the complaint is not covered by the policy, but a "lesser included claim" may be covered by the policy. Ferguson v. Birmingham Fire Ins. Co., 254 Or 496, 460 P2d 342 (1969).

d.   **Claims Not Asserted in Complaint**

There is a duty to defend if allegations in the complaint would support a covered claim, even if the claim is not plainly stated in the complaint. Holloway v. Republic Indemnity Co. of Am., 201 Or App 376, 119 P3d 239 (2005) (overruled on other grounds by Holloway v. Republic Indemnity Co. of Am., 341 Or 642, 147 P3d 329 (2006)).

e.   **Declaratory Judgment Actions**

Declaratory Judgment Actions are very limited in Oregon prior to the resolution of the primary claim. ORS 183.310.

f.   **Settlement**

The duty to defend an insured includes the duty to settle the case within the policy limits if it would be reasonable to do so. ORS 746.230(1).

4.   **Duty to Pay**

The duty to indemnify is determined by the factual outcome of the case against the insured. This is a narrower obligation than the duty to defend.

5.   **Overlapping Coverage**:

a.   When a trial court enters judgment in a case involving multiple insurers, the plaintiff is entitled to receive full recovery for the loss up to the limits of the liability of the insurers who are subject to the judgment.

b.   *Generally, liability insurance follows the car and the driver's policy excess. If there is difficulty in determining which insurer's insurance is valid and collectible, "the court is faced with determining which company shall be considered primarily liable, or treating the 'other insurance' clause in each insurer's policy as so repugnant that they must both be ignored, and apply the rule that the loss shall be equally prorated between them." Lamb-Weston, Inc. v. Oregon Auto. Ins. Co., 219 Or 110, 119, 341 P2d 110 (1959).*

     c.   When apportioning the award among multiple insurers, the court cannot consider the liability limits for any insurers who have previously settled or are otherwise not subject to the court's judgment. *Cascade Corp. v. American Home Assurance Co.,* 206 Or App 1, 135 P3d 450 (2006).

6.   Third-Party Bad Faith

The carrier will be held liable for an excess judgment if it failed to exercise due care. Additional damages may be recoverable if certain circumstances apply. *Goddard ex rel. Estate of Goddard v. Farmers Ins. Co. of Oregon,* 173 Or App 633, 22 P3d 1224 (2001).

B.   PERSONAL INJURY PROTECTION (FIRST PARTY)

1.   Mandatory Coverage

     a.   PIP is required in every passenger motor vehicle insurance policy as prescribed by statute with a maximum deductible of $250. ORS 742.524(2).

     b.   An insurer may provide more favorable benefits than prescribed by law. ORS 742.532.

     c.   PIP benefits cover the insured, resident members of the insured's household, passengers and pedestrians struck by an insured. ORS 742.526.

     d.   Permissive drivers of a motor vehicle are entitled to PIP benefits under the motor vehicle owner's policy. *See Sheptow v. Geico General Ins.,* 240 Or App 18, -- P3d --- (2011) (*Note: It appears the Court misinterpreted the statute, and this matter will likely be petitioned to the Oregon Supreme Court*).

2.   Use of Vehicle

PIP benefits are triggered when an insured's injury results from the "use, occupancy or maintenance of any motor vehicle." ORS 742.520(2).

In determining what constitutes "use" of a motor vehicle, Oregon courts have looked to whether there was a "consequential nexus" between the use of the vehicle and the injuring event. PIP benefits are unavailable for persons injured only as a result of a "but for" connection between the use of the motor vehicle and the resulting injury. Takata v. State Farm Mut. Auto. Ins. Co., 217 Or App 454, 176 P3d 415 (2008).

3.   Exclusions

Insurer may deny PIP benefits to any injured person who:

a.   Uses a motor vehicle that is owned, furnished, or regularly used, and the vehicle is not described in the policy;

b.   Was operating a motorcycle or moped which is not owned by the injured person;

c.   Was not operating a private passenger vehicle as defined by ORS 742.520(7);

d.   Intentionally causes self-injury;

e.   Participates in organized racing or speed contest;

f.   Is injured as a pedestrian in an accident outside this state, other than the insured person or a member of the insured person's family residing in the same household; or

g.   "Willfully conceals or misrepresents any material fact in connection with a claim for PIP benefits." ORS 742.530.

4.   Benefits

a.   **Minimum Required Benefits**

i.   Medical: $15,000 for reasonable and necessary medical, hospital, dental, surgical, ambulance and prosthetic service.

Note: With the exception of hospital charges, the amount paid to a provider shall not exceed the maximum allowed under the Oregon Workers Compensation system. However, PIP insurers are required to pay at least 90% of hospital charges. ORS 742.524.

ii.   Wage loss: a PIP eligible claimant who is usually engaged in a remunerative occupation (i.e., a job that pays), but because of a motor vehicle accident is unable to perform that occupation for at least 14 days, is allowed to receive 70% of his or her lost income or $3,000 per month, whichever is less. The Oregon legislature recently amended ORS 742.524 and extended the maximum recoverable amount from $1,250 per month to $3,000 per month (or 70%, whichever is less) for policies issued or renewed on or after January 1, 2010. Any claims for PIP benefits under policies not issued or renewed on or after January 1, 2010 are limited to the $1,250 per month maximum. This benefit is also subject to a maximum payment period in the aggregate of 52 weeks.

iii. Funeral: All reasonable and necessary funeral expenses incurred within one year after the date of the injuries, not to exceed $5,000.

iv. Child Care: If injured person is a parent of a minor child and is required to be hospitalized for a minimum of 24 hours, $25 per day for child care, not to exceed $750. ORS 742.524.

b. **Calculating PIP Benefit to the Insured**

> i. *PIP benefits stack. Anti-stacking provisions are unenforceable in the context of PIP benefits. See Anderson v. Farmers Ins. Co. of Oregon, 188 Or App 179, 71 P3d 144 (2003).*

ii. PIP benefits may be reduced or eliminated when the injured person is entitled to receive workers' compensation benefits or any other similar medical or disability benefits. ORS 742.526.

iii. Denial of Benefits. All medical expenses shall be deemed reasonable, unless the insurer gives notice of denial of charges within 60 days from receipt of an invoice. ORS 742.528 (this is generally a rebuttable presumption).

iv. Insurance companies are prohibited from denying any claim (including PIP) without first conducting a "reasonable investigation based on all available information." ORS 746.230(1)(d). In some circumstances, a "reasonable investigation" will include and IME. *Ivanov v. Farmers Ins. Co. of Oregon*, 344 Or 421, 430, 185 P3d 417 (2008).

> *Note: PIP insurers are statutorily authorized to audit the quality and need for medical care once services are provided. ORS 742.520(7)(b).*

v. Proof of Loss. The definition of "proof of loss" for PIP benefits is "documentation that allows an insurer to determine whether a person is entitled to personal injury protection benefits and the amount of any benefit that is due." ORS 742.518.

Note: If PIP benefits are paid based on information that appeared to establish proof of loss, but is later determined that the insurer was not responsible for the payment, a medical provider to which the payment was sent must immediately repay the insurer upon receiving notice and explanation of the incorrectly issued PIP payment. ORS 742.529.

5. Disputes with an Insured

a. Binding Arbitration

i. PIP disputes between insurer and insured are decided by arbitration if parties mutually agree to arbitration at the time of the dispute. ORS 742.520(6). There is no compulsory binding arbitration nor is a three-person panel required for PIP dispute arbitrations.

ii. PIP arbitrations must be conducted under the local court rules in the county where the arbitration is held. ORS 742.521.

iii. Arbitration must occur within a reasonable time after requested by the insured.

iv. Insurer pays the cost of the arbitration, except for $100, which is paid by the claimant. The insurer is not required to pay attorney fees or costs related to production of evidence. ORS 742.522.

v. The binding effect of arbitration is limited to the findings and awards to the parties of the arbitration, but not for other litigation. ORS 742.521.

b. Litigation

Insured can file a lawsuit against the insurer if arbitration is not agreed upon. Attorney fees shall be recoverable within six months of the proof of loss unless the insurer notifies the insured in writing of the following:

i. That the insurer accepts coverage and restricts the dispute to the amount of benefits due the insured.

ii. That the insurer consents to resolve the case with binding arbitration. *See Proposed Forms, Appendix 2.* ORS 742.061.

Note: The Oregon Court of Appeals held that despite sending a letter consenting to coverage, if an insurer denies one or more of a claimant's medical bills, the insurer has not actually consented to coverage under ORS 742.061 and therefore may be still liable for the claimant's attorney fees. Badrick v. Farmers, 238 Or App 320, 242 P3d 685 (2010).

Note: The Oregon Supreme Court has held that there is no requirement under ORS 742.061 that a "proof of loss" be in writing; an oral notice can be sufficient. Parks v. Farmers Ins. Co., 347 Or 374, 227 P3d 1127 (2009).

      c.   **No First Party Bad Faith**

There is no exposure beyond the policy limits without a separate, independent tort (e.g. intentional infliction of severe emotional distress). Absent a separate tort, the insured is not entitled to emotional distress or punitive damages under the contract.

      6.   **PIP Reimbursement**

Subject to certain limitations, all authorized motor vehicle liability insurers may be required to directly reimburse the PIP carrier.

      a.   **PIP Provider Reimbursement Options**:

          i.   Seek reimbursement for the PIP benefits they have paid directly from the negligent party's carrier via inter-insurer reimbursement. ORS 742.534;

          ii.   Seek reimbursement by attaching a lien to any action filed by the injured person against the negligent party. ORS 742.536; or

          iii.   Exercise their right of subrogation against any settlement or judgment the injured party receives from the negligent party. ORS 742.538.

Note: Under ORS 742.534, an insurer who does not seek reimbursement via inter-insurer reimbursement <u>may only</u> recover PIP payments under the provisions of ORS 742.536 (the lien statute) or ORS 742.538 (the subrogation statute). Both statutes have to be strictly followed and both require the insurer to pay its proportionate share of the injured party's costs and fees incurred as part of the injured party's action for recovery.

Note: Subrogation under ORS 742.538 is only available to a health insurer if subrogation recovery through inter-insurer reimbursement under ORS 742.534 or lien under ORS 742.536 is not available. Providence Health Plan v. Winchester, 252 Or App 283, --- P3d ---- (2012). Additionally, any provision in a health insurance policy requiring the insured to reimburse the health insurer is void. Providence Health Plan v. Winchester, 252 Or App 283, --- P3d ---- (2012).

      b.   If insurers are signatories to an inter-insurer agreement under ORS 742.534 and the dispute among the insurers involves reimbursement, the insurers may be limited to recovery via inter-insurer arbitration. *California Cas. Indem. Exch. v. Federated Mut. Ins. Co.*, 251 Or. App. 371, --- P3d ---- (2012).

c. The ability of a PIP carrier to obtain reimbursement is limited to the extent that the amount recovered exceeds the economic damages. ORS 742.544; *Gaucin v. Farmers Ins. Co.*, 209 Or App 99, 146 P3d 370 (2006).

d. There will be no reimbursement in the event the liability carrier has exhausted its policy limits to the claimant. *Farmers v. American Fire & Casualty Co.*, 117 Or App 347, 844 P2d 235 (1992).

e. The insurers must arbitrate the disputes of liability or the amount of recovery. This is a statutory requirement that can be accomplished through Arbitration Forums in the event both carriers are signatories. If they are not signatories, arbitration must be accomplished independently.

f. If insured does not file a lawsuit, a PIP insurer can file a lawsuit in the insured's name. ORS 742.534.

C. UNDERINSURED/UNINSURED MOTORIST COVERAGE (FIRST PARTY)

1. Uninsured Motorist (UM)

a. Insurer will pay to the insured all "damages" that the insured is legally entitled to recover because of bodily injury sustained by the operator of an uninsured motor vehicle. ORS 742.504. Punitive damages are not recoverable.

b. With an Identified Motorist, UM protection applies when:

    i. The motorist has no collectible automobile bodily injury liability insurance or bond; or

    ii. The writing insurance company of the motorist denies coverage thereunder; or

    iii. If the motorist's insurance company declares bankruptcy or for which a receiver is appointed or becomes insolvent; or

    iv. If the identity of the motorist cannot be determined, it shall be a disputable presumption that a vehicle is uninsured in the event that the insured and insurer, after reasonable efforts, fail to discover within 90 days from the date of the accident, the existence of a valid and collectible automobile bodily injury liability insurance or bond applicable at the time of the accident. ORS 742.504.

c. Additional requirements when the identity of the motorist cannot be determined:

i.   ***Hit and Run***: When the insured is involved in a hit-and-run accident, the insured must:

    1)   Report the accident within 72 hours to the authorities in the state where the accident occurred;

    2)   Within 30 days, submit a statement under oath that the insured or the legal representative of the insured has a cause or causes of action arising out of such accident for damages against a person or persons whose identity is unascertainable, and setting forth the facts in support thereof; and

    3)   At the insurer's request, the insured or legal representative of the insured makes the vehicle occupied at the time of the accident available for inspection. ORS 742.504.

ii.   ***Phantom Vehicle***: When the insured is injured by a phantom vehicle that has no physical contact with the insured or the vehicle, the insurer must:

    1)   Corroborate the facts with competent evidence other than the testimony of the insured or any person having an uninsured motorist claim resulting from the accident; and

    2)   Report the accident within 72 hours to the appropriate authorities in the state where the accident occurred; and

    3)   File with the insured within 30 days thereafter a statement under oath that the insured or the legal representative of the insured has a cause or causes of action arising out of such accident for damages against a person or persons whose identity is unascertainable, and setting forth the facts in support thereof. ORS 742.504.

2. Underinsured Motorist Coverage (UIM)

> a. *UIM coverage is available when: (1) UM policy limits equal the liability limits of the at-fault driver's policy; and (2) the amount of liability insurance recovered is less than UIM coverage. ORS 742.502(5).*
>
> b. *The important factor in determining whether a UIM claim exists is the amount paid, not the amount of the limits. See Takano v. Farmers Ins. Co. of Oregon, 184 Or App 479, 56 P3d 491 (2002).*

c. UIM coverage is available when one of the following exhaustion requirements has occurred:

    i. The limits of liability have been exhausted by payment of judgments or settlements to the injured person or other injured persons;

    ii. The limits have been offered in settlement, the insurer has refused consent, and the insured protects the insurer's right of subrogation to the claim against the tortfeasor;

    iii. The insured gives credit to the insurer for the unrealized portion of the described liability limits as if the full limits had been received if less than the described limits have been offered in settlement, and the insurer has consented to the settlement; or

    iv. The insured gives credit to the insurer for the unrealized portion of the described liability limits as if the full limits had been received if less than the described limits have been offered in settlement. If the insurer has refused consent, the insured protects the insurer's right of subrogation to the claim against the tortfeasor. ORS 742.504(4)(d).

    v. Insurers must pay insureds up to the limit of their UIM policy when the insured sustains an injury from an accident with an underinsured vehicle, even if the vehicle was owned by a public body or operated by an employee who is subject to the Tort Claims Act (ORS 30.260-ORS 30.300). The UIM statute requires insurers to provide coverage that will pay "all sums that the insured is legally entitled to recover" from the owner of an uninsured and underinsured vehicle that causes the bodily injury to the insured. Any limits by the Tort Claims Act will not reduce what an injured insured is legally entitled to recover. ORS 742.504(1)(a).

3. **Calculation of Benefits in UM and UIM**

a. UM/UIM coverage is primary when an insured occupies his or her own vehicle. When an insured occupies a vehicle he or she does not own, UM/UIM coverage is excess to the extent it exceeds primary coverage (*i.e.* non-stacking). ORS 742.504(9).

b. Payments from the liability insurer or tortfeasor reduce the UM/UIM benefits. ORS 742.504. The fact that an insured's total damages exceed the UM policy limits is irrelevant in the calculation of benefits. *Vogelin v. American Family Mut. Ins. Co.*, 346 Or 490, 213 P3d 1216 (2009). The insured is not entitled to a recovery that exceeds his or her contracted UM coverage. *Id.*

c. *In the case of overlapping coverage, payments from another insurer reduce the UM/UIM benefits. Pitchford v. State Farm Mut. Auto. Ins. Co., 147 Or App 9, 934 P2d 616 (1997).*

d. An offset for amounts payable under workers compensation may be taken from the claimant's total damages, but not from the UM/UIM policy limits. *Bergmann v. Hutton,* 337 Or 596, 101 P3d 353 (2004).

e. In order to recover on a UIM claim, the underinsured driver's liability policy limits must be less than the claimant's UIM policy limits. Mid *Century Ins. Co., v. Perkins*, 344 Or 196, 179 P3d 633 (2008).

f. PIP offset: Subtract PIP from damages (the true value of the injury, which includes economic and noneconomic loss).

g. Injured parties may collect from their UM/UIM coverage if they are injured by a self-insured vehicle if the amount they recover from the self-insurer is less than the UM/UIM liability limit of their own policy. ORS 742.502(6).

h. UIM benefits are calculated by subtracting the insured's recovery of other automobile liability policies from the insured's UM policy limit. *Country Cas. Ins. Co. v. Villa-Chavez*, 228 Or App 677, 208 P3d 1036 (2009). In instances where the tortfeasor's policy limits are apportioned among multiple persons, a UIM insurer may only subtract the portion received by its insured. *Id.*

> i. *By statute, Oregon allows for UM anti-stacking provisions in automobile insurance policies. ORS 742.504(9). In order to effectively prevent UM stacking, insurers must incorporate the statutory language into their policies. Policy provisions which purport to prevent stacking, but use language that differs from the statute, may be held to allow for UM stacking. Country Mutual Ins. Co. v. White, 212 Or App 323, 157 P3d 1212 (2007).*

D. DISPUTES WITH THE INSURED IN UM/UIM

1. Binding Arbitration

a. UM/UIM disputes between insurer and insured are decided by arbitration if mutually agreed upon. There is no compulsory binding arbitration. ORS 742.504(10).

b. Parties must use a three-person binding arbitration panel for all UM/UIM claims unless parties agree to different process. The arbitration must be conducted under the local court rules in the county where the arbitration is held. ORS 742.504.

c. Initiating formal arbitration proceedings is extremely informal. A claimant seeking UM coverage may use any type of written document, including a faxed-cover letter, that uses language that clearly and expressly provides a message, notice, offer, or demand for arbitration. *Luka v. Tri-Met,* 244 Or App 565, 261 P3d 44 (2011).

2. Litigation

a. Attorney fees are recoverable within six months from the date proof of loss is filed with an insurer and an action is brought in court unless the insurer notifies the insured in writing of the following:

    i. The insurer accepts coverage and restricts the dispute to liability and the amount of damages due the insured.

    ii. The insurer consents to binding arbitration. *See* proposed forms in Appendix 3 & 4. ORS 742.061.

Note: Insurers seeking protection from attorney fees under the safe harbor provisions of ORS 742.061 will be denied protection if they challenge whether damages are due in a claim; the safe harbor provisions only allow challenges to the amount of damages due. Badrick v. Farmers, 238 Or App 320, 242 P3d 685 (2010).

Note: The Oregon Supreme Court recently held that an insurer's letter to a UIM claimant, in which the insurer consented to arbitration of a UIM claim if a dispute arose, did not "formally institute arbitration" within two years pursuant to Oregon's ORS 742.504(12), and thus, the UIM claim was time-barred. As a result of this ruling, if by consenting to arbitration of a UIM claim an insurer wishes to protect itself from an attorney fee claim under ORS 742.061, the insurer's consent must be unconditional. Bonds v. Farmers, 349 Or 152, 240 P3d 1086 (2010).

While the majority didn't address this issue, the dissent expressed concern that the Court's holding necessarily implies that if an insurer wants to avoid the threat of an attorney fee award, it must unconditionally consent to arbitration, and render the 2-year time limitation of ORS 742.504(12) void. Id.

Note: ORS 742.061 does not require a "proof of loss" be in writing; oral notice can be sufficient. Parks v. Farmers Ins. Co., 347 Or 374, 227 P3d 1127 (2009).

          b.   Recent Oregon Court of Appeals broadened definition of "proof of loss" in UIM context. The 6-month time clock under ORS 742.061 begins to count when an insurer has: (1) notice of an accident; (2) knowledge that the insured was significantly injured; (3) knowledge that the alleged at-fault driver had liability insurance; and (4) knowledge that the insured has UIM coverage. *Hall v. Speer,* 244 Or App 392, 261 P3d 1259 (2011).

                    i.   While more may be required, the UIM insurer should, at a minimum ask the liability carrier, the at-fault party, and the insured's attorney for the amount of the at-fault's liability policy limits to determine whether a UIM obligation may exist. *Id.*

     3.   **No First Party Bad Faith**

There is no exposure beyond the policy limits unless a separate, independent tort is established (e.g. intentional infliction of severe emotional distress). Absent a separate tort, the insured is not entitled to emotional distress or punitive damages under the contract.

WASHINGTON
PERSONAL LINES

I.   WASHINGTON PROCEDURE

A.   STATUTE OF LIMITATIONS

Washington statutes of limitations vary depending upon the claims asserted.

Action	Time Limitation	Source
Claim for Use and Occupation of Property	6 years.	RCW 4.16.040(3)
Injury to Real Property for Waste/Trespass	3 years.	RCW 4.16.080(1)
Injury to Personal Property (car)	3 years.	RCW 4.16.080(2)
Negligent Bodily Injury	3 years.	RCW 4.16.080(2)
Libel, Slander	2 years.	RCW 4.16.100(1)
Intentional Injury (assault & battery)	2 years.	RCW 4.16.100(1)
Construction Ultimate Repose	6 years from the date of completion. (Breach of written construction contracts - 6 years from substantial completion regardless of discovery).	RCW 4.16.310; RCW 4.16.326(1)(g) *1000 Virginia Limited Partnership v. Vertecs Corp.*, 158 Wash 2d 566, 146 P3d 423 (2006).
Contribution	1 year from judgment or settlement.	RCW 4.22.050(3)
Actions Against Public Entities (except for claims involving injuries from health care)	The action must be presented to the entity. The plaintiff must then wait at least 60 calendar days before filing suit (the statute is tolled during that time period). The plaintiff will have the same statute of limitations as the theory of recovery.	RCW 4.92.110 and RCW 4.96.020
Actions Against Dissolved Corporations	2 years - if the corporation was dissolved before June 7, 2006. 3 years - if the corporation was dissolved after June 7, 2006.	RCW 23B.14.340 *Ballard Square Condo. Owners Ass'n. v. Dynasty Const. Co.*, 158 Wash 2d 603, 146 P3d 914 (2006).
Product Liability	3 years from discovery (or should have discovered) of injury.	RCW 7.72.060(3)

Wrongful Death	The claim is governed by the theory of recovery – *i.e.,* negligent injury, intentional injury, product liability, etc.	*White v. Johns-Manville Corp.*, 103 Wash 2d 344, 693 P2d 687 (1985).
Contract /UM/UIM	6 years from the breach (normally considered the time the claim is denied by the insurer).	RCW 4.16.040; *White v. Johns-Manville Corp.*, 103 Wash 2d 344, 693 P2d 687 (1985).
General/ "Catchall"	2 years.	RCW 4.16.130; *Mayer v. City of Seattle*, 102 Wash App 66, 10 P3d 408 (2000).

B.   TOLLING (EXTENDING) THE STATUTE OF LIMITATIONS

1. Absence from the state or concealment will toll the statute of limitations during the absence.

2. Person under 18 – tolled until reach age 18. RCW 4.16.190.

3. Person disabled or incompetent—tolled until disability passes. RCW4.16.190.

4. Death of plaintiff – personal representative can bring claim outside the normal statute, but no longer than one year from death. RCW 4.16.200.

5. If a claimant lacks a lawyer, an insurer shall give notice to first party claimants thirty (30) days, and to third party claimants sixty (60) days before the expiration of the statute of limitations. WAC 284-30-380(5).

6. The period of a service-member's military service may not be included in computing time limits for statute of limitations purposes. The provision applies to actions filed in both federal and state court. 50 U.S.C. App. § 526.

C.   COMMENCING THE ACTION

An action is commenced once the summons and complaint are both filed with the court and served on the defendant. The plaintiff has the option to file first, then serve, or serve first and then file. Plaintiff has 90 days to achieve the second step and have the act relate back to the original file or service date. RCW 4.16.170. Amending a complaint will not extend the time to complete service. *Banzeruk v. Howlitz*, 132 Wash App 942, 135 P3d 512 (2006).

D. SERVICE METHODS

1.   Generally, service of an individual in Washington is required to be made by personal service. RCW 4.28.080(14).

2.   **Substitute Service is Permitted** – leaving a copy of the summons and complaint at the usual abode of the individual with a person of suitable age. This requires follow up mail service. The follow up mail is required to be "First Class." RCW 4.28.080(14), (15).

3.   **Motor Vehicles** – There is a special method of service for operators of motor vehicles. Non-residents of the state automatically appoint the Secretary of State of Washington as their agent for service of process. Likewise, if a resident subsequently leaves the state, the Secretary of State is appointed as the agent for service. Plaintiff only needs to show there was a mailing of the summons and complaint by registered mail, return receipt requested, to the last known address of the defendant. Plaintiff must file an appropriate affidavit of those efforts. RCW 46.64.040.

E. APPEARANCE BY THE DEFENDANT

1.   A defendant who lives in Washington has 20 days to file an answer to the plaintiff's complaint. CR 4(a)(2).

2.   A defendant who lives outside the state has 60 days. RCW 4.28.180.

F. COURT SYSTEMS IN WASHINGTON

1.   **Levels of Courts in Washington**

  a.   There are four main levels of courts in Washington: 1) courts of limited jurisdiction; 2) superior courts; 3) the court of appeals; and 4) the Supreme Court.

2.   **Courts of Limited Jurisdiction**

  a.   **These Courts Are Also Known as "District" or "Municipal" Courts.**

These courts can hear non-felony criminal cases and disputes involving claims under $50,000. Excluding parking infractions, 7 out of every 8 cases filed in state courts are filed at this level.

  b.   **Discovery in District Court is Limited**. (CRLJ 26)

    1)   Limited Interrogatories – Permitted questions can relate to damages, the identity of persons with

knowledge of liability; persons with knowledge of damages; and the identity of experts expected to testify. In addition, a party can request two additional sets of interrogatories, with 20 or fewer questions each.

2) Limited Request for Documents – Permitted requests include: a copy of an insurance agreement; copies of agreements or contracts that are the subject of the dispute; copies of bills for special damages; and 5 additional types of documents or things to be chosen by the discovering party.

3) Limited Depositions – All parties are permitted to be deposed; two additional persons may be deposed by each party.

4) Limited Requests for Admissions – Each party is permitted to serve up to 15 written requests for admissions.

5) No other discovery is permitted without leave of the court.

6) Time – Discovery is commenced no earlier than 21 days after service of the summons and complaint. All discovery must be completed within 60 days of the requests or 90 days of service of the summons and complaint, whichever is longer.

c. Appeals are to the superior court in the same county as the district court. RALJ 2.3(a).

d. Clark County cases will not be placed on the trial readiness calendar of a district court or superior court until a party files a "Notice to Set for Trial" and the other party does not object or its objections are overruled.

3. **Superior Court**

a. There is no limit on the types of civil and criminal cases that a superior court can hear, so these courts are called "courts of general jurisdiction."

b. All superior courts are grouped into single or multi-county districts. There are 30 such districts in Washington State. Counties with large populations usually comprise one district, but in less-populated areas, a district may consist of two or more counties.

c. The Washington Court Rules govern discovery in superior court cases. In addition, each district has extensive local rules that supplement the procedure rules, including supplements on filing of motions and rules governing discovery.

d. In most cases, superior court decisions can be appealed to the Appellate Court. In some cases, however, the decisions can be appealed directly to the Supreme Court.

4. Appellate Court

a. Most cases that are appealed from the superior court go directly to the Court of Appeals. The Court of Appeals must hear every case that is appealed.

b. On appeal, the court can reverse the decision (*i.e.*, overrule it), modify the decision, affirm it (*i.e.*, agree with it), or remand it (*i.e.*, send it back to the superior court for a new trial).

c. The Appellate Court issues two main types of decisions: 1) published opinions; and 2) unpublished opinions. If the opinion is unpublished, it cannot be cited and is not binding authority on the court. GR 14.1. Unpublished opinions are useful, however, because they can indicate the mindset of the justices on the bench.

5. Supreme Court

a. The Supreme Court is Washington's highest court.

b. Generally, cases come to the Supreme Court from the Appellate Court. However, direct Supreme Court review of a trial court's decision is permitted if: the action involves a state officer, a trial court has ruled a statute or ordinance unconstitutional, conflicting statutes or rules of law are involved, or the issue is of broad public interest and requires a prompt and ultimate determination.

c. The Supreme Court must hear cases involving the death penalty. In all other cases, the Court can decide whether or not it wants to hear the appeal.

G. ADR - COURT MANDATED ARBITRATION

1. Mandatory arbitration is required in all counties with a population of more than 150,000. In counties with a population of 150,000 or less, mandatory arbitration may be authorized by a majority vote of the superior court judges of the county or by local legislative authority. RCW 7.06.010.

> 2.   *In all counties, cases involving claims of less than $15,000 are subject to mandatory arbitration. RCW 7.06.020. Counties may, upon a vote of the superior court judges, increase the limit from $15,000 to $50,000. RCW 7.06.020.*

3.   If a party is not happy with the results of an arbitration, the party may appeal the decision within 20 days after the award is filed with respect to that party. MAR 7.1(a); *McKee v. Simmerly*, 120 Wash App 217, 84 P3d 919 (2004).

H.   SPECIAL PLEADING RULES

> 1.   *Washington is a "notice pleading" state. In other words, a plaintiff's allegations need only put the defendant on notice of the general claim.*

2.   It is improper to plead general damages. RCW 4.28.360. Defendant is permitted to request a statement of damages.

> 3.   *Counterclaims and cross-claims are compulsory – e.g., if the insured has a claim against the plaintiff that arises out of the same occurrence, the claim must be brought or it will be waived.*

I.   DISCOVERY METHODS

1.   There are five basic methods of discovery in Washington.

     a.   **Request for Production** – request for documents from the other parties.

     b.   **Interrogatories** – written questions to be answered and signed under oath.

     c.   **Depositions** – in Washington, this includes the discovery of experts who are expected to testify at trial.

     d.   **Request for Admissions** – this is the fourth and often forgotten method of discovery. It requests the opposing party to admit facts or the legal effect of facts.

     e.   **Independent Medical Examinations** – if the mental or physical condition of a person is at issue, the opposing party is permitted to seek an independent medical examination.

         i.   The rule specifically allows for the person being examined to have a representative present.

ii. The party or representative may make an audio tape recording of the examination. It may also be videotaped if there is an agreement between the parties or a court order.

II.   WASHINGTON BASICS OF LIABILITY AND TORT

A.   MOTOR VEHICLE AND PEDESTRIAN DUTIES

1.   Auto

a. Vehicles approaching intersections – if two vehicles approach at the same time, the vehicle on the left must yield to the vehicle on the right. RCW 46.61.180(1). This favored position is not absolute; all drivers still have the duty to exercise ordinary care and to remain observant to avoid an accident.

b. Deception doctrine – when a favored driver deceives a reasonably prudent, disfavored driver into thinking that he can safely make a left turn, the deceiving driver will be found to be at fault for the accident. *Hammel v. Rife*, 37 Wash App 577, 682 P2d 949 (1984).

c. No person shall turn a vehicle or move right or left upon a roadway unless and until such movement can be made with reasonable safety and is made upon the giving of an appropriate signal. Every driver has the obligation to give a signal before turning. RCW 46.61.305(1).

d. Drivers turning left must yield to opposing traffic. RCW 46.61.185.

e. U-turns are proper only if they can be made safely. RCW 46.61.295.

f. A driver cannot enter an intersection unless there is proper room on the other side – *i.e.,* no blocking intersection. RCW 46.61.202.

g. Vehicles entering a public road from a private drive must yield to the traffic on the public road. RCW 46.61.205.

h. Vehicles coming from an alley, driveway or building in a business district must stop before entering the sidewalk. Right-of-way belongs to pedestrians and to traffic on the public road. RCW 46.61.365.

i. Stop signs must be obeyed, and right of way belongs to those in the intersection or those vehicles so close to the intersection that it would constitute an immediate hazard. RCW 46.61.190.

j. Yield Signs – vehicles must slow down, and if required, stop.

k.   Negligence as a matter of law: In *Niven v. MacDonald*, 72 Wash 2d 93, 431 P2d 724 (1967), the Supreme Court held that regardless of whether a driver is favored or disfavored, he has a duty to look out for approaching traffic. Failure to see a plainly visible oncoming car constitutes negligence as a matter of law. *Id.* at 727-728.

2.   **Auto v. Pedestrian**

a.   Every driver of a car shall exercise reasonable care to avoid an accident with a pedestrian. RCW 46.61.245. Despite this statute, the driver and the pedestrian have a duty to exercise reasonable care to the safety of themselves and others.

b.   Pedestrians are subject to the direction of traffic control devices. RCW 46.61.230.

c.   Pedestrians must walk on sidewalks where available, and where none are available, on the left side of the road facing traffic. RCW 46.61.250.

d.   Crosswalks are a prolongation of a sidewalk. RCW 46.04.160.

Note: the law imposes a higher duty of care for drivers approaching persons in wheelchairs and blind pedestrians (evidenced by canes or seeing eye dogs) in crosswalks. This means that drivers "are required to take all necessary precautions to avoid injury to these individuals," and drivers who fail to take such precautions are liable in damages for any injury caused to such an individual. RCW 70.84.040.

3.   **Auto v. Animal**

a.   Washington has open and closed/restricted ranges.

b.   The driver has a duty to look out for range animal crossing roads in an open range.

c.   Statutes make it unlawful for a person to cause or allow livestock to stray upon a public road in a closed or restricted range. RCW 16.24.070.

4.   **Use of Seat Belts and Child Passenger Restraints**

a.   Washington requires all persons within the state to exercise the use of a seat belt while traveling in a car. RCW 46.61.688.

b.   Washington requires children be restrained in a child restraint system until the child is eight years old or is 4' 9" or taller. RCW 46.61.687.

c.   The driver of a vehicle transporting a child who is under thirteen years old shall transport the child in the back seat positions in the vehicle where it is practical to do so. RCW 46.61.687.

d.   Failure to use a seat belt cannot be introduced at trial to prove comparative fault of the injured person. In addition, evidence of a driver's failure to properly seat belt children into a car cannot be used affirmatively to prove negligence against the driver for the child's injuries.

5.   **Citations**

a.   *Generally, courts will not allow evidence that an individual was issued a citation involving a traffic infraction during an automobile accident to be admitted at trial. Billington v. Schaal, 42 Wash 2d 878, 259 P2d 634 (1953).*

   i.   *However, if a civil defendant pleads guilty to the infraction, the evidence of the citation and the plea can be entered as an admission against the defendant. It also has impeachment value. Ryan v. Westgard, 12 Wash. App 500, 530 P2d 687 (1975).*

B.   **CLAIMS BETWEEN FAMILY MEMBERS & CLAIMS AGAINST CHILDREN**

1.   **Spousal Immunity** – Washington has abolished spousal immunities.

2.   **Children** – a child 4 years old or younger cannot be held negligent.

3.   **Parent/Child**

a.   **Vicarious liability** – Vicarious liability is not normally imputed to the parent for the negligence of the child.

b.   **Negligent supervision of a child** – A parent may be found liable if: (1) a child has dangerous proclivities; (2) the parents know or should know of child's dangerous proclivities; and (3) the parent fails to exercise reasonable care to control the child. Allowing a minor to possess a gun does not, by itself, establish evidence to support a negligent supervision claim. *Schwartz v. Elerding*, 166 Wash.App. 608, 270 P3d 630 (2012).

For example, in *Schwartz v. Elerding*, 166 Wash.App. 608, 270 P3d 630 (2012), seventeen year-old Joey Elerding got his father's truck stuck in the Schwartzes' driveway. When Mr. Schwartz came to investigate, an altercation ensued.

Joey grabbed an unloaded 20-guage shotgun from a toolbox in the truck and struck Mr. Schwartz in the face with it causing him severe injuries. Mr. Schwartz learned that Joey's parents gave him the shotgun and allowed him to store it in the truck. The Schwartzes sued for negligent supervision and negligent entrustment alleging that the Elerdings knew or should have known of the dangerous proclivity of all minors in possession of a gun. The Court concluded that a minor merely possessing a gun does not, by itself, establish that the minor has a dangerous proclivity.

c.   **Family Car Doctrine** – A parent is liable for the negligent conduct of a family member if: (1) the car is owned, provided or maintained by the parent or other family member; (2) the car is for the customary conveyance of family members and other family business; (3) at the time of the accident, the car is being driven by a member of the family for whom the car is maintained; and (4) the car is being driven with the express or implied consent of the parent.

For example, in Kaynor v. Farline, 117 Wash App 575, 72 P3d 262 (2003), a son got into a car accident, and the other driver sued the parents. The court held that a reasonable jury could conclude that the father was liable under the family car doctrine because the father bought the car for his son, paid the insurance, the son was the exclusive driver of the vehicle, the son drove himself to school, work and to visit his father. Thus, the court concluded the car was a convenience to the family.

d.   **Parental Immunity** – Previously, the parental immunity doctrine operated as a nearly absolute bar to suit in Washington by a child for personal injuries caused by a parent, no matter how wrongful the parent's conduct. Zellmer v. Zellmer, 164 Wash 2d 147, 154, 188 P3d 497 (2008). However, while parent-child immunity has not been completely abolished by the Washington courts, it has been limited. For example, in Merrick v. Sutterlin, 93 Wash 2d 411, 610 P2d 891 (1980), the Washington Supreme Court held that a minor child injured by the negligence of his parent in an automobile accident has a cause of action against that parent. Id. at 416. But the Merrick court left open other issues of parent-child immunity, holding "[w]e recognize that there may be situations of parent authority and discretion which should not lead to liability" and acknowledging that rather than absolutely abrogating parent-child immunity, issues of immunity should be approached on a case-by-case basis. Id.

i.   Washington courts have consistently held that doctrine of parental immunity precludes liability for negligent parental supervision, but not for a parent's wanton or willful failure to supervise a child. *Zellmer v. Zellmer*, 164 Wash 2d 147, 150-51, 188 P3d 497 (2008).

Note: When parental immunity does apply, it has been applied to protect step-parents to the same extent as biological or adoptive parents, as long as the step-parent stands "in loco parentis" (in the place of the parent), i.e., step-parents who are obligated to support step-children under the family support statute. Zellmer v. Zellmer, 164 Wash 2d 147, 151, 188 P3d 497 (2008).

C.   NEGLIGENCE CLAIMS

1.   Reasonable Care

Washington requires persons to use reasonable care to avoid injury to others. The law requires a person to conform his or her conduct to a particular standard toward another. That standard is the reasonably prudent person standard.

2.   Negligence Per Se

Generally, a violation of a statute is evidence of negligence and not negligence per se. *See Morse v. Antonellis*, 149 Wash 2d 572, 70 P3d 125 (2003) (court held that even if a party violates a statute, whether the defendant acted reasonably or negligently, was a question for the jury. By holding the defendant liable as a matter of law, the court would be substituting the jury's judgment for its own.) However, violating certain statutes regarding electrical fire safety, the use of smoke alarms, sterilization of needles and instruments used in body piercing, body art, tattooing, electrology, precautions against spreading disease or driving under the influence of alcohol or drug *will* be considered negligence per se. RCW 5.40.050.

3.   Negligent Infliction of Emotional Distress

In *Hunsley v. Girard*, the Washington Supreme Court held that plaintiff, whose home was struck and invaded by a defendant's car outside of plaintiff's immediate presence and without immediate physical impact to her, had a viable cause of action to recover for physical heart damage resulting from emotional distress, despite no physical impact to her. Plaintiff could recover if her mental distress was the reaction of a reasonable person and was manifested by objective symptoms. 87 Wash 2d 424, 436, 553 P2d 1096 (1976).

In *Hegel v. McMahon,* 136 Wash 2d 122, 960 P2d 424 (1998), the Washington Supreme Court held that a family member is permitted to recover for negligent infliction of emotional distress if they are present at the accident scene. This presence at the scene need not be at the time of the accident. In fact, the relative could arrive at the scene after the accident. *Id.* at 132. However, while there is no "bright line" rule as to how soon after an accident a family member must observe a relative's injuries to state a claim for negligent infliction of emotional distress, the observation must be immediate enough to observe injuries such as "the crushed body, the bleeding, the cries of pain, and in some cases, the dying words."

Additionally, the emotional distress must be related to observing the traumatic injuries rather than the expected emotions related to the unanticipated death of a family member. *Colbert v. Moomba Sports, Inc.,* 163 Wash 2d 43, 176 P3d 497 (2008). Finally, a family member who arrives at the scene of an accident after receiving a phone call informing them of an accident's occurrence, does not arrive at the scene of an accident "unwittingly," thus, they cannot maintain a claim for negligent infliction of emotional distress. *Ko v. Seaview Chevrolet,* 156 Wash App 1055, ---P3d--- (2010) (This is an unpublished opinion. It cannot be cited as authority to a court of law.)

As for the necessary proof of damage, the court requires a showing of "objective symptomology." *Hegel* at 135. The plaintiff's emotional distress must be susceptible to medical diagnosis and proved through medical evidence. *Id.* There must be objective evidence of the severity of the distress, and a causal link between the observations at the scene and the subsequent emotional reaction. Nightmares, sleep disorders, intrusive memories, fear, and anger may be sufficient. For these symptoms to satisfy the objective symptomology requirement, they must constitute a diagnosable emotional disorder.

4. Liability of a Vehicle Owner:

Permissive use of a vehicle does not automatically impute liability on the owner, unless one of the following applies:

        a.   **Family Purpose Doctrine**: The family purpose doctrine applies when: (1) the owner furnished the vehicle for the customary conveyance of member(s) of his immediate family, (2) the operator was a member of his immediate household, (3) the vehicle was operated with the acquiescence or permission of the owner, and (4) the accident or injury occurred within the area of the permissive use. *Pflugmacher v. Thomas*, 34 Wash. 2d 687, 209 P.2d 443 (1949).

        b.   **Negligent Entrustment:** A person who entrusts a vehicle to a non-owner may be liable under a negligent entrustment theory if that person knew, or should have known, that the person to whom the vehicle was entrusted is heedless, reckless, or incompetent. *Mejia v. Erwin*, 45 Wash. App. 700, 726 P.2d 1032 (1986).

        c.   **Agency or Joint Enterprise** exists, such as an employment relationship.

D.   WASHINGTON RESIDENTIAL LANDLORD TENANT ACT

        1.   The Washington Residential Landlord Tenant Act, RCW Chapter 15.18, is a separate section of the RCW dedicated to defining the duties of residential landlords and tenants and any remedies available to the parties. RCW 59.18, *et seq.*

2.   *Washington requires landlords to maintain premises in a manner that is fit for human habitation. This includes complying with applicable codes, maintaining the floors, roofs, walls, chimneys, fireplace, and structural components; keeping the property safe from conditions that would cause fire; providing programs for pest control; providing adequate locks; maintaining electrical, plumbing, and heating; keeping the structure reasonably watertight; and providing working smoke detectors. RCW 59.18.060.*

3.   The Washington Residential Landlord Tenant Act, in contrast to Oregon's Residential Landlord Tenant Act, does not provide a specific statute of limitations for claims brought under its scope. Therefore, any claims brought by a landlord or tenant pursuant to the Act must adhere to the time limitations set forth by the applicable common law causes of action (negligence, contract, etc.).

4.   When a landlord has ownership interest in a property and is required to obtain and maintain insurance for a condominium building, Washington law presumes that the tenants inside the condominiums are considered co-insureds under the policy absent any agreement to the contrary. Thus, the insurer cannot sue the tenant to recover amounts paid out under the policy. *Community Assoc. Underwriters of America, Inc., v. Kalles et al,* 164 Wash App 30, 259 P3d 1154 (2011).

5.   A landlord's tenants are coinsureds under the landlord's policy for the entire building, not only the unit the tenant occupies. *Trinity Universal Insurance Co. v. Cook,* 1 68 Wash.App. 431, 276 P3d 372 (2012).

6.   A tenant's spouse not residing on the property or a named tenant is also considered a coinsured under the landlord's insurance policy. *Id.*

E.   PREMISES LIABILITY

1.   Defining the Entrant

A landowner's duty of care to persons on his or her land is governed by the entrant's common law status: invitee, licensee, or trespasser. *Cultee v. City of Tacoma,* 95 Wash App 505, 977 P2d 15 (1999).

a.   **Invitee** – Washington case law recognizes two classes of invitees – business visitors and public invitees. A public invitee is a person who is invited to enter or remain on land as a member of the public for a purpose for which the land is held open to the public. A business invitee is a person who is invited to enter or remain on land for a purpose directly or indirectly connected with business dealings with the possessor of the land.

b. **Licensee** – A licensee is one who enters real property with the possessor's permission or tolerance for the licensee's own purpose or business rather than for the possessor's benefit. A social guest comes under the definition of a licensee. Permission to enter the premises can be either express or implied.

c. **Trespasser** – A trespasser is one who enters the premises of another without invitation or permission. An invitee or licensee may fall to the status of a trespasser if he exceeds the scope of the possessor's invitation.

2. Duty

a. **Invitees** – Of the three classifications – invitee, licensee, and trespasser – the highest duty of care is owed to invitees. A landowner is subject to liability for physical harm caused to his invitees by a condition on the land if the landowner knows of, or by the exercise of reasonable care would discover, the condition, and should realize that it involves an unreasonable risk of harm to such invitees; the invitee would not discover or realize the danger, or will fail to protect themselves against it; and fails to exercise reasonable care to protect them against the danger. *Ford v. Red Lion Inns*, 67 Wash App 766, 770, 840 P2d 198 (1993).

b. **Licensee** – A landowner owes a licensee a duty to prevent the entrant from suffering harm due to a condition on the land that is known or should have been known to the landowner, that would cause an unreasonable risk of harm to the licensee; and the licensee did not discover the condition and would have no reason to know of the condition. *Tincani v. Inland Empire Zoological Soc.*, 124 Wash 2d 121, 133, 875 P2d 621 (1994).

c. **Trespasser** – A landowner generally does not owe a trespasser a duty of care, except to refrain from willfully or wantonly injuring the trespasser. *Ochampaugh v. City of Seattle*, 91 Wash 2d 514, 518, 588 P2d 1351 (1979).

d. **Contractors as Possessors of Land** – If a contractor creates a dangerous condition on land and a harm occurs while the contractor is engaged in his work, the contractor is subject to the same premises liability as a landlord would be. *Williamson v. The Allied Group*, 117 Wash App 451, 72 P3d 230 (2003).

F.   DOG BITE

1.   Strict Liability

Washington does not follow the "one-bite rule" (i.e., every dog owner has one "free bite" before civil liability can be imposed). In Washington, if a dog bites a person while the person is in a public place or lawfully in a private place (including the dog owner's property) the owner of the dog shall be liable for damages, regardless of the prior viciousness of the dog or owner's knowledge of the viciousness of the dog. RCW 16.08.040. However, proof of provocation of the attack by the injured person is a complete defense against any cause of action for damages. RCW 16.08.060.

Note: RCW 16.08.040 is limited to when a dog bites "a person."

G.   TIMBER TRESPASS

1.   Washington has a statutory cause of action if a person removes or injures a tree on another person's land. RCW 64.12.030.

2.   Treble damages are recoverable. RCW 64.12.030.

3.   Defendant can mitigate to single damages upon a showing that the trespass was casual or involuntary, due to a belief that the property was their own. RCW 64.12.040.

H.   LIQUOR LIABILITY

1.   Commercial hosts

Commercial hosts will be liable for injuries to third persons if the host serves an "obviously intoxicated" person or an "apparently intoxicated" person and the person served causes injury. RCW 66.44.200; Barrett v. Lucky 7 Saloon, 152 Wash 2d 259, 96 P3d 386 (2004). Commercial hosts are also liable for injuries to third persons if they serve a minor person. The commercial host is also liable for foreseeable injuries to any person, including the minor, as a result of serving the minor.

2.   Quasi–Commercial Hosts

Quasi-commercial hosts are held to the same standard so long as the service of alcohol was for the benefit of the quasi-commercial host – *e.g.*, company party.

3.   Social Hosts

Social hosts are not held to the same standard as commercial hosts. However, social hosts will be liable for serving intoxicants to a minor.

I. WRONGFUL DEATH - RCW 4.20.005 *et seq.*

1. The personal representative (PR) of a deceased is permitted to bring a cause of action for the wrongful death of the deceased.

2. The action is brought on behalf of designated beneficiaries. The action is for the spouse, children and stepchildren of the deceased. If there are none, then for the parents or siblings who were dependent on the deceased.

3. There is no limit to the amount of damages. A jury is permitted to award any amount it deems just.

4. Regardless of being survived by statutorily defined beneficiaries, a decedent's estate is entitled to recover economic damages the decedent would have been entitled to recover had they survived, but non-economic damages can only be recovered by statutory beneficiaries. *Wilson v. Grant,* 162 Wash App 731, 258 P3d 689 (2011).

5. Damages are for the "pecuniary loss" suffered by the beneficiaries, including the monetary contributions that would have been received, loss of support, services, love, affection, care, companionship, society, and consortium. There is not a permissible damage for the grief or sorrow of the beneficiaries.

6. The actions of the deceased survive to the PR and against the PR. Due to this, there is also recovery for the pain and suffering of the deceased prior to death.

7. The contributory fault of the deceased will be imputed to the claimant of the wrongful death action. RCW 4.22.020.

8. Death of a child – parents have a direct action for death of child that they depended on for support. RCW 4.24.010. *Armantrout v. Carlson,* 141 Wash App 716, 170 P3d 1218 (2007) (overruled on other grounds, *Armantrout v. Carlson,* 166 Wash 2d 931, 214 P3d 914 (2009)).

J. SHARING THE FAULT

1. Comparative Fault

Washington is a pure comparative fault state. The fault of the plaintiff will be considered, and will reduce the amount of recovery. However, it will never bar recovery. RCW 4.22.005.

2. Fault of an Intoxicated Plaintiff

This is an exception to the pure comparative fault standard. If a plaintiff's intoxication causes their injury or death, and a jury finds that the intoxicated person is more than 50% at fault, then the intoxicated plaintiff is barred from recovery. RCW 5.40.060. This also applies to actions involving minors against social hosts.

3. Multiple Defendants

a. **Several Liability** – Typically, each defendant is only liable for his share of the total fault to the plaintiff.

b. **Joint Liability** – There will be joint liability between parties to the action if the injury is not divisible, the defendants acted in concert, or the plaintiff was not at fault for any of the injury.

   i. As a general rule, a negligent defendant cannot be held jointly liable for another defendant's intentional conduct. However, the court in *Tegman v. Accident & Medical Investigations, Inc.,* concluded that a negligent defendant can only be held jointly and severally liable for damages resulting from negligence, not for intentional conduct committed by others. 150 Wash 2d 105, 75 P3d 497 (2003).

4. Multiple Tortfeasors and Trial

The jury will consider the fault of all "entities," and apply fault up to 100%. An "entity" is defined as the plaintiff/claimant or injured person for whom recovery is sought, defendants, third party defendants, entities released by the plaintiff, entities with any other individual defense against the claimant, and entities immune from liability. RCW 4.22.070.

a. The effect of the statute is to make all those with possible fault considered by the jury no matter if they are present in the lawsuit.

b. Therefore, when a plaintiff settles with a party, the plaintiff takes the risk that the entity will be found more at fault than reflected in the settlement.

5. Contribution

A right of contribution exists between persons who are jointly and severally liable. You cannot seek contribution against a party who is immune from liability to the plaintiff.

Note: the calculation of contribution is the comparative fault of the party compared to the other parties.

6.   Indemnity

Indemnity has been abolished, except by contract. RCW 4.22.040(3). The sole action is contribution, which still allows for full recovery against a third entity.

K.   DAMAGES PRINCIPLE IS TO MAKE THE PERSON WHOLE

1.   Special Damages

a.   **Personal Property** – If the property is destroyed, the measure of damages is the difference between the fair market value of the property before destruction and its fair market value after destruction. If the property is not destroyed or damaged beyond repair, the measure of damages is:

   i.   The reasonable value to repair plus any diminished value that remains after the repair; or

   ii.   The difference in the value of the property value without the repair. Washington also permits loss of use damages associated with damaged or destroyed personal property.

b.   **Real Property** – If real property is destroyed, a jury can choose to award damages based on the lost fair market value of the property *or* the reasonable cost of repair and/or rebuilding. *Thompson v. King Feed & Nutrition Service, Inc.*, 153 Wash 2d 447, 105 P3d 378 (2005).

c.   **Lost Earnings and Lost Earning Potential**

   i.   Lost earnings are the amount of damages the person lost in wages as a result of the accident minus any mitigation.

   ii.   Earning potential arises from a permanent injury that prevents the person from going back to work or limits the person's ability to work.

d.   **Medical Damages** – a person is entitled to recover for medical bills. These are the reasonable and necessary medical expenses (past, present and future) that are a result of the injury.

2. General Damages

Pain and suffering as well as emotional distress.

3. Punitive Damages

Punitive damages prohibited in Washington except as expressly authorized by legislation. Fluke Corp. v. Hartford Accident & Indem. Co., 145 Wash 2d 137, 34 P3d 809 (2001). Punitive damages have been held to not be available under common law bad faith actions. Barr v. Interbay Citizens Bank of Tampa, Fla., 96 Wash 2d 692, 635 P2d 441 (1981).

4. Treble Damages

Treble damages are damages that are three (3) times the amount that the fact-finder determines is owed.

    a.   *The Consumer Protection Act (CPA) allows insureds to obtain treble damage "punishment" awards, subject to a statutory limit of $25,000. RCW 19.86.09*

    b.   *The Insurance Fair Conduct Act (IFCA) allows insureds to obtain limitless treble damages. RCW 48.30.015(3).*

5. Pre-Judgment Interest

Pre-judgment interest is only allowed on claims for fixed sums, or where the damages can be computed without reliance on opinion or discretion.

    a.   Caveat: If a defendant appeals a liability verdict but does not appeal the issue of damages, a plaintiff may be entitled to pre-judgment interest as of the date the verdict was rendered. For example, in *Hadley v. Maxwell*, 120 Wash App 137, 84 P3d 286 (2004), plaintiffs sued defendants for injuries they suffered during an automobile accident. In 1998, a jury concluded that defendants were liable and awarded plaintiffs $136,000 in damages. After an appeal on the liability issue only, the defendants were granted a new trial in 2003. The 2003 jury concluded that defendants were liable. Plaintiff proposed a judgment of $136,000 plus pre-judgment interest as of the 1998 verdict. The court held that because the defendant did not dispute the damages award when it appealed the liability issue only, pre-judgment interest was proper.

6. Attorney Fees

Attorney fees are only recoverable when there is a contract or statute that allows recovery.

a. In any damages action pleaded by the prevailing party for $10,000 or less (exclusive of costs), the court will allow, as part of costs of the action, attachment of the prevailing party's reasonable attorney fees. RCW 4.84.250.

b. In an action for pleaded damages of $10,000 or less, the plaintiff, or party seeking relief, is deemed the prevailing party when the recovery (exclusive of costs) is equal to or greater than a settlement offer made by the plaintiff or party seeking relief. RCW 4.84.260.

c. In an action for pleaded damages of $10,000 or less, the defendant, or party resisting relief, is deemed the prevailing party when plaintiff's recovery (exclusive of costs) is zero or in an amount less than defendant's settlement offer. RCW 4.84.270.

d. Offers to settle must be done pursuant to court rule and served on the opposing party at least 10 days prior to trial, but no earlier than 30 days after service and filing of the summons and complaint. RCW 4.84.280.

Note: The Washington Court of Appeals held that for purposes of seeking attorney fees under RCW 4.84.250-280, a mandatory arbitration is considered the equivalent of a "trial" and settlement offers must be presented ten days prior in order to invoke the statute. Williams v. Tilaye, 158 Wash App 1001, --- P3d ---- (2010), rev. granted 171 Wash 2d 1019, 253 P3d 393 (2011 (This opinion has not been published; it cannot be cited to as authority to a court of law and review by the Washington Supreme Court has been granted.)

L. SETTLEMENT

The Washington legislature intended to encourage settlement while ensuring full compensation of tort victims when it enacted the pure comparative fault system.

1. Reasonableness Hearings

Reasonable Hearings are required when there are multiple tortfeasors and the claimant is attempting to enter into a release, covenant not to sue, or covenant not to enforce a judgment or similar agreement.

a. 5 days notice – All parties entering into a release, a covenant not to sue or similar agreement must provide 5 days written notice of the intent to enter the agreement with all parties and the court. A copy of the proposed agreement must accompany the notice.

b. Hearing will be had with all parties able to present evidence. The burden of proof regarding the reasonableness of the settlement is on the party requesting the settlement. The court will determine if the amount paid is reasonable.

c. A reasonableness hearing can be had prior to entry of final judgment of the action upon motion of a party. RCW 4.22.060(1).

2. Settlement Offers

Just because an insurer does not extend a settlement offer equal to the highest appraisal value, does not mean the insurer is acting in bad faith so long as the lower settlement offers are supported by evidence and other appraisals. *Lloyd v. Allstate Ins. Co.*, 167 Wash. App. 490, 275 P.3d 323 (2012).

3. Discharge of Contribution Claims

The affect of a release, covenant not to sue, or similar agreement is to release the settling entity from all liability for contribution. The claim of the releasing party is reduced by the amount of the settlement unless the court finds the amount was unreasonable, then the amount the claim is reduced by is the amount the court determines to be reasonable. RCW 4.22.060(2).

a. If a court finds the settlement unreasonable, it does not affect the validity of the settlement. Instead, it only affects the amount the claim is reduced by. RCW 4.22.060(3).

4. Settlement with a Minor

Washington Courts require approval of settlements involving a minor or incapacitated person. SPR 98.16W.

a. A settlement guardian must be appointed. A report must be conducted and opinion provided to the probate court for approval of the settlement.

b. Only certain persons can act as a settlement guardian. They must have had 5 years practice as an attorney, have no conflict of interest, and meet certain requirements (e.g., certification).

5. All Material Terms

A settlement agreement remains unenforceable until both parties have agreed upon the material terms of the settlement agreement. *Veith v. Xterra Wetsuits, LLC*, 144 Wash App 362, 183 P3d 334 (2008).

6. **Attorney Fees**

The Washington Supreme Court recently held that an agreement to settle "all claims" pursuant to RCW 4.84.250-.280 encompasses all claims, including claims for attorney fees. McGuire v. Bates, 169 Wash 2d 185, 190-91, 234 P3d 205 (2010).

M. **BANKRUPTCY BY CLAIMANTS**

1. **Failure to Declare**

Failure to declare is where a bankruptcy petitioner fails to list an insurance claim as an asset in the bankruptcy filing, he or she may be prevented from later pursuing that claim under the doctrine of judicial estoppel. A bankruptcy trustee will generally not be barred from pursuing the personal injury claim on behalf of the bankruptcy creditors. *Arkinson v. Ethan Allen, Inc.*, 160 Wash 2d 535, 160 P3d 13 (2007). However, failing to disclose the insurance claim properly will likely not result in a similar bar. *Baldwin v. Silver*, 147 Wash App 531, 196 P3d 170 (2008).

2. **Value of Claim**

The doctrine of judicial estoppel does not apply to limit recovery in a personal injury action where the plaintiff had previously listed the claim as an asset, but severely undervalued it. However, the bankruptcy valuation can be introduced to a jury in a personal injury suit to prove any later higher claims are excessive. *Ingram v. Thompson*, 141 Wash App 287, 169 P3d 832 (2007).

III. **WASHINGTON BAD FAITH CLAIMS**

A. **STATUTORY BAD FAITH CLAIMS (FIRST PARTY)**

1. **RCW 48.01.030**

Washington requires insurers to act in good faith. RCW 48.01.030. Violation of this statute may give rise to a tort action for bad faith. *Smith v. Safeco Ins. Co.*, 150 Wash 2d 478 (2003); *American States Ins. Co. v. Symes of Silverdale, Inc.*, 150 Wash 2d 462 (2003).

    a.   In *Coventry v. Am. States Ins. Co.*, the Washington Supreme Court held that an insurer could, and did in this case, violate its duty of good faith and fair dealing, despite the finding of no coverage. 136 Wash 2d 269, 285, 961 P2d 933. Specifically, an insured may maintain an action against its insurer for bad faith investigation of the insured's claim and violation of the Consumer Protection Act regardless of whether the insurer was ultimately correct in determining coverage did not exist. *Id.* at 279. The court also held that the insured was entitled to make a claim for those amounts and damages normally associated with bad faith and Consumer Protection Act (CPA) violations. *Id.* at 285.

2.   **Washington Consumer Protection Act** (CPA)

CPA also provides a private right of action. RCW 19.86. A violation of RCW 48.01.030 has been held to be a *per se* violation of the CPA. *Levy v. North American Co. for Life & Health Ins.,* 90 Wash 2d 846, 586 P2d 845 (1978).

      a.   **Attorney Fees** – CPA provides for reasonable attorney fees. RCW 19.86.090.

3.   **Insurance Fair Conduct Act** (IFCA)

IFCA provides recovery for actual damages for first party claimants who are unreasonably denied a claim for coverage or payment of benefits. RCW 48.30.015.

>   a.   ***Treble Damages** – Under RCW 48.30.015, a court, in its discretion, may increase any actual damages award up to three times the amount (with no cap) upon finding that an insurer acted unreasonably in denying a claim for coverage or payment of benefits or has violated one of five insurance regulations:*

      i.   Specific unfair claims practices. WAC 284-30-330;

      ii.   Misrepresentation of policy provisions. WAC 284-30-350;

      iii.   Failure to acknowledge pertinent communications. WAC 284-30-360;

      iv.   Standards for prompt investigation. WAC 284-30-370;

      v.   Standards for prompt, fair and equitable settlements. WAC 284-30-380.

4.   **Mandatory Attorney & Expert Witness Fees**

> *After finding a violation, IFCA requires an award of reasonable attorney fees and actual and statutory litigation costs, including expert witness fees.*

5.   **Notice of IFCA Claim**

A claimant must provide 20 days written notice to both the insurer and the state's Office of the Insurance Commissioner before filing suit under the law. Notice may be provided by regular mail, registered mail, or certified mail. Notice under the statute is deemed received three (3) business days after mailing, and the statute of limitations for the action is tolled during the 20 day notice period. The notice must provide for the basis of the cause of action, however, if the insurer does not resolve the claim during the 20-day period, the claimant may bring suit without further notice.

B.   COMMON LAW ACTIONS FOR BAD FAITH (FIRST PARTY)

1.   Insurers have a common law duty to act in good faith toward their insureds. Breach of the duty of good faith gives rise to an independent tort action which is separate from the insurance contract. The common law duty of an insurer to act in good faith has been held to be quite broad and "may be reached by conduct short of intentional bad faith or fraud." *Griffin v. Allstate Ins. Co.,* 108 Wash App 133, 29 P3d 777 (2001).

C.   THIRD PARTY BAD FAITH

1.   *Bad Faith or Negligent Refusal to Settle – Third party claimants may not pursue a private cause of action for breach of good faith under a liability policy, pursuant to a statute or the Unfair Claims Practices Regulations unless the party is the Insurance Commissioner of the State of Washington. Tank v. State Farm Fire & Cas. Co., 105 Wash 2d 381, 715 P2d 1133 (1986); Smith v. Safeco Ins. Co., 150 Wash 2d 478 (2003). However, Washington insureds may assign their right to a bad faith claim to a third party. Safeco v. Butler, 118 Wash 2d 383, 823 P2d 499 (1992).*

2.   Assignment usually occurs in the context of a stipulated settlement where the insured agrees to assign his rights against the insurer to a third party in exchange for a covenant signed by the third party not to execute the judgment (likely an excess verdict) against the insured.

3.   Excess judgment – a judgment awarded to an injured party that exceeds the insured's policy limits. If the cause of the excess verdict is the insurer's bad faith or negligence (most commonly in refusing opportunity to settle within policy limits) the remedy is generally the amount of the excess judgment, in addition to:

a.   Interest on the excess judgment.

b.   Emotional distress suffered as a direct result of the insurer's tortious failure to settle.

D.   ADDITIONAL REMEDIES

1.   In addition to the remedies listed above, recovery under a claim for bad faith may also include economic loss due to the denial of

the claim – *i.e.,* losses suffered because the insured was not able to meet his/her business or personal responsibilities.

2.   Bad faith claims can exist solely for procedural errors (e.g., untimely communication). However, damages under such a claim will not be presumed and are limited. The claimant (first or third party) has the burden of proving "actual harm." *St. Paul Fire and Marine Ins. Co. v. Onvia, Inc.*, 165 Wash 2d 122, 196 P3d 664 (2008).

3.   Even if a court finds bad faith, no damages will be awarded unless the claimant has suffered a harm stemming from the act of bad faith. *Ledcor Industries, Inc. v. Mutual of Enumclaw Insurance Co.*, 150 Wash App 1, 206 P3d 1255 (2009) (*rev den.* 167 Wash 2d 1007, 220 P3d 209 (2009)) (Mutual of Enumclaw stood ready to pay its share of Ledcor's defense costs and funded the eventual settlement with the third party; Ledcor ultimately received what it was entitled to under the policy and suffered no compensable harm, thus, no damages were awarded for that claim).

IV.   WASHINGTON BASICS OF AUTO INSURANCE LAW

A.   LIABILITY INSURANCE (THIRD PARTY)

1.   Financial Responsibility Law (FRL)

RCW 46.29.490 requires every driver to have liability insurance with the following minimum limits:

     a.   *BI – $25,000/$50,000*

     b.   *PD – $10,000*

     c.   Reporting requirements – unless a motor vehicle accident is investigated by a law enforcement officer, drivers involved in a motor vehicle accident must report within 4 days of the accident if there is an injury or property damage above $700. RCW 46.52.030.

2.   Exclusions

     a.   **Age Exclusions** – Courts have found exclusions for persons under 25 and under 21, other than the named insured, valid despite the Financial Responsibility law.

     b.   **Intra-Family Exclusions** – In *Mutual of Enumclaw v. Wiscomb*, 97 Wash 2d 203, 643 P2d 441 (1982), Maura Wiscomb was injured in a collision between her motorcycle and an automobile driven by her husband. Mutual of

Enumclaw provided both liability and uninsured motorist coverage for the Wiscomb vehicles. Maura Wiscomb initiated a lawsuit against her husband alleging personal injuries as a result of his negligence. The trial court found that the insurer was relieved of its obligation under the family or household exclusion clause of the insurance contract. The Court of Appeals reversed, holding exclusion clauses which purport to deny coverage to family or members of the household violated state public policy of assuring compensation to the victims of negligent and careless drivers. *Id.* at 213.

In response, some carriers are writing limited exclusions to their policies. These provisions limit intra-family recovery to the financial responsibility law limits. Instances where the policy provided household member coverage and the individual insureds and insurers later contracted for the exclusion has yet to be addressed by the courts. However, voluntary declination of coverage by the insured has been found to not violate public policy in one instance. The court upheld a motorcycle insurance policy provision excluding liability coverage for claims made by passengers where the insured intentionally rejected that coverage when it was offered to the insured. *Progressive Casualty Ins. Co. v. Jester*, 102 Wash 2d 78, 683 P2d 180 (1984).

c. **Permissive User Exclusion** – Washington policies are generally written so that they exclude coverage to those who do not reasonably believe they have permission to drive the vehicle. The standard is an objective test. Courts have found that if the individual knew he was not to operate the car or had no reasonable grounds to believe he could operate the car, then the exclusion is enforceable.

d. **Exclusions for Carrying Persons or Property for a Fee**
These are permissible. In one instance, a woman agreed to do her friend's laundry and errands for a week in exchange for gas money. An accident occurred, the court found the exclusion applicable, and excluded coverage.

e. **Non-Resident Members of Household** – Residency often determines whether an individual is an insured under a policy. Residency typically refers to the place where a person has a permanent intention to reside or live. The courts have established factors to be used in determining whether a person can be classified as a resident of a household.

In *GMAC v. Grange Ins. Co.*, 38 Wash App 6, 684 P2d 744 (1984), the Court of Appeals held that to determine whether a "part time" person is a member of a household requires an examination of the circumstances involved in each case. The court must look to the: (1) intent of the part time resident; (2) degree of formality of the relationship between the part-time resident and the remaining members of the household; (3) proximity of living quarters; and (4) whether the part-time resident has another place of lodging. Weight will be given to the intention of the part-time resident as to whether his sleeping and eating away from the household is permanent or temporary. Finally, any policy ambiguities will be interpreted in favor of coverage. *Id.* at 10.

f.   **Intentional Acts**

  i.   Most insurance policies exclude coverage for the intentional acts of their insureds. At issue is whether the act is classified as intentional or accidental. In *Allstate v. Bauer*, 96 Wash App 11, 97 P2d 617 (1999), the court held that for purposes of insurance coverage, an accident is "an unusual, unexpected, and unforeseen happening." *Id.* at 15. Thus, because the insured deliberately shot the victim, the insured's mistaken belief that the victim was armed did not constitute an accident, even though the shooting was in self defense. *Id.*

  ii.   Although the undefined term "accident" in an insurance policy generally excludes intentional and deliberate acts, if there is an additional, unexpected, independent or unforeseen event that influenced the intentional act resulting in damages, an insurer has a duty to defend. *State Farm Fire & Cas. Co. v. Kwing On Ng*, 160 Wash App 1039, --- P3d ---- (2011). (*Note: this is an unpublished opinion and cannot be cited as authority, and is only demonstrative of how the court approaches the issues involved in this case).*

  iii. If an insured files for bankruptcy and then commits some intentional act, the intentional act exclusion does not prevent the bankruptcy trustee from collecting under the insured's policy. *See American States Ins. Co. v. Symes of Silverdale, Inc.*, 150 Wash 2d 462, 78 P3d 1266 (2003) (holding that although the policy had an intentional act exclusion, the trustee was entitled to recover for property damage because: 1) the trustee acquired all the insured's property interests, including insurance policies, as of the date of the bankruptcy; and 2) a debtor's wrongdoing is not attributable to the trustee.)

g.   **Effect on Additional Insured**

If a policy has an exclusion related to "the insured," the exclusion may not necessarily apply to an additional insured. For example, in *Truck Ins. Exchange v. BRE Properties*, 119 Wash App 582, 81 P3d 929 (2003), a subcontractor purchased an insurance policy that listed the general contractor as an additional insured. The insurance policy excluded coverage for employees of "the insured." One of the subcontractor's employees was injured while working on the project and brought a lawsuit against the general contractor. The insurance company denied coverage, arguing that the policy excluded coverage for employees of the insured. On appeal, the court concluded that the general contractor was entitled to coverage because the policy excluded coverage for "the insured" not "an insured." Here, the employee was employed by the subcontractor – not the general contractor.

3.   **Duty to Defend**

Duty to defend is broader than duty to pay/indemnify.

> a.   *General Rule – the duty to defend a lawsuit is determined by the allegations of the plaintiff's complaint. Insurers are required to defend any suit which alleges facts, which if proven, would render the insurer liable under the terms of the policy, even if the allegations could be false. Unless the claims are clearly not covered under the policy, an insurer's duty to defend will be triggered. Woo v. Fireman's Fund Ins. Co., 161 Wash 2d 43, 164 P3d 454 (2007).*

b.   The complaint is liberally construed in favor of finding coverage. *Dickins v. Stiles,* 81 Wash App 670, 673, 916 P2d 435 (1996) (*rev. denied,* 129 Wash 2d 1029 (1996)). Notice Pleading – sometimes it is necessary to look beyond the complaint due to the type of pleading allowed in Washington. This gives rise to a carrier's duty to investigate the underlying facts before it can refuse to defend.

> c.   *One must go beyond the complaint if (1) the allegations are in conflict with the facts already known or (2) the allegations are ambiguous. In any event, the carrier must investigate further before refusing to defend. E-Z Loader Boat Trailers, Inc. v. Travelers Indemnity Co., 106 Wash 2d 901, 908, 726 P2d 439 (1986); McMahan & Baker, Inc. v. Continental Cas. Co., 68 Wash App 573, 580, 843 P2d 1133 (1993).*

d. Declaratory Actions to Avoid Duty to Defend – While not completely settled, the Court of Appeals indicates that a declaratory action may be proper. *Western Nat'l. Assur. Co. v. Hecker*, 43 Wash App 816, 821 n.1, 719 P2d 954 (1986). *But see Travelers Ins. Co. v. North Seattle Christian & Missionary Alliance*, 32 Wash App 836, 650 P2d 250 (1982) (holding declaratory actions are not permitted to avoid duty to defend). However, the carrier cannot pursue the declaratory action prior to the trial of the tort action if the facts establishing a defense to coverage would also establish the insured's liability in the underlying case.

e. Coverage Litigation – If successful, the insured will be entitled to the benefit of the coverage, and attorney fees. If the insurer fails to defend and it is later determined that it should have defended, the insurer must pay the attorney fees the insured incurred in the defense, and may also be required to indemnify, depending on the fact determination in the underlying case. If the failure to defend was the result of an insurer's bad faith action, the insurer may be estopped from denying coverage. *See Mutual of Enumclaw Ins. Co. v. Dan Paulson Const.*, 161 Wash 2d 903, 924, 169 P3d 1 (2007) (holding that policy's exclusion was void as a result of insurer's bad faith conduct in attempting to engage in improper communication with the arbitrator). At this point, although the insurer will not be responsible for an excess verdict against the insured, arguably the insured may have an IFCA bad faith claim against the insurer. *See* "Washington Bad Faith Claims," *supra*.

4. Duty to Pay

The duty to indemnify is determined by the factual outcome of the case against the insured. This is a narrower obligation than the duty to defend.

a. Reservations of Rights – the insurer will often accept the duty to defend by reserving the right of indemnification. If the reservation is not timely made, the carrier can waive the right to deny coverage.

b. At the first indication that the claim may be outside the scope of coverage, the carrier should immediately send a reservation of rights letter. Washington does not require any particular form. The letter need only make it clear that the carrier is preserving it rights to contest liability under the terms of the policy.

c. Each and every ground that the carrier relies on for the reservation must be set out. If new reasons come to light during the litigation, an updated reservation letter should be sent.

5. Right to Participate

The right to defend includes the right to participate. Thus, even though the insured may not want the insurance company to participate in a trial against a tortfeasor, the insurance company may still do so. See Peterson-Gonzalez v. Garcia, 120 Wash App 624120 Wash App 624, 86 P3d 210 (2004).

6. Defense Under a Reservation of Rights

In Tank v. State Farm Fire and Casualty Co., 105 Wash 2d 381, 715 P2d 1133 (1986), the Supreme Court held that the insurer did not breach its duty of good faith by accepting a tendered defense under a reservation of rights and subsequently, refusing to pay the judgment against the insured. The court also held that insurers have an enhanced duty when defending an insured under a reservation of rights. This enhanced duty has five requirements. First, the insurer must thoroughly investigate the cause of the accident and the nature and extent of plaintiff's injuries. Second, the insurer must retain competent counsel for the insured. Third, the insurer has the responsibility of fully informing the insured not only of the reservation of rights defense, but of all developments relevant to his policy coverage and the progress of his lawsuit. Fourth, the insurer must refrain from favoring its own monetary position over the insured. And fifth, defense counsel must solely represent the insured, and cannot partake in action detrimental to the insured. Id. at 387-388.

Subsequent decisions have expanded on this holding. In *Safeco v. Butler*, 118 Wash 2d 383, 823 P2d 499 (1992), the Court held that a showing of harm is an essential element of an action for bad faith handling of an insurance claim. *Id.* at 389. Further, the courts will now impose a rebuttable presumption of harm once the insured meets the burden of establishing bad faith. *Id.* at 390.

Note: When seeking a declaratory action, an insurer must take caution to avoid demonstrating a greater concern for its own monetary interest over the insured's financial risk. When defending an insured under a reservation of rights, an insurer may be found in bad faith when pursuing a declaratory action if the insurer's actions place the insured at financial risk. Mutual of Enumclaw Ins. Co. v. Dan Paulson Const., 161 Wash 2d 903, 169 P3d 1 (2007). See "Washington Bad Faith Claims," supra.

7. Settlement

An insurer that disputes coverage cannot compel an insured to forego a settlement that is in the insured's best interest. For the purposes of a court's determination as to whether a negotiated settlement without an insurer's blessing is reasonable, allegations or a formal finding of bad faith on the part of the insurer are not necessary. *Martin v. Johnson,* 141 Wash App 611, 170 P3d 1198 (2007).

a. **Multiple Tortfeasors** – In a case involving joint tortfeasors, a settlement that includes a release or covenant not to sue requires a court hearing to determine whether the proposed settlement is reasonable, or to determine what would be reasonable. In the event of a finding of unreasonableness, nothing prohibits the parties from modifying their settlement to conform to what the court determined would be reasonable. *Meadow Valley Owners Association v. St. Paul,* 137 Wash App 810, 156 P3d 240 (2007).

8. **Overlapping Coverage**

On certain occasions, more than one policy will apply to provide liability coverage in a particular occurrence. For example, when an individual has an accident while driving a friend's car, he may have his own insurance policy and the individual who loaned the car may also have a policy. The question becomes which policy pays the first dollar of any settlement or judgment?

a. **Pro Rata Clauses** – limits the insurer's liability to its "pro rata" share of the loss under the combined limits of the policies involved.

b. **Excess Clauses** – limits the insurer's liability to the amount over any other collectible insurance.

i. When two insurance policies provide coverage to an insured and both policies have excess coverage clauses at the same coverage level, those clauses cancel each other out and both insurers are liable for a pro rata share of the judgment. *Safeco Ins. Co. of Illinois v. Country Mutual Ins. Co.,* 2011 WL 5043487 (Wash App 2011) (*Note: this is an unpublished opinion and cannot be cited as authority, and is only demonstrative of how the court approaches the issues involved in this case*).

c. **Escape Clauses** – provides coverage only if no other coverage is available.

d. **"Other Insurance" Clauses** – Washington courts favor applying the "other insurance" clauses when possible – *i.e.,* comparing the multiple policies' "other insurance" clauses and determining how they fit together.

e. **Pro Rata v. Excess** – generally the pro rata policy is deemed to be primary, and the excess policy will be excess.

f. **Excess v. Excess, Escape v. Escape** – the policy provisions will be repugnant and disregarded. Washington requires each insurer to contribute the same amount until the liability of the smaller policy is exhausted. The remaining carrier then pays the balance until its limits are exhausted or the liability is paid.

9. Negligence Claims Arising from Another Insured's Intentional Torts

Generally, an insured's negligence liability for failing to prevent another insured's intentional act is excluded from liability insurance coverage by a policy exclusion for bodily injury arising as a result of the intentional acts of "an insured." *Farmers Ins. Co. v. Hembree*, 54 Wash App 195, 733 P2d 105 (1989). In *Hembree*, the Washington Court of Appeals held that the policy at issue clearly and unambiguously excluded coverage for bodily injury "arising as a result of intentional acts of <u>an insured</u>." The claim of negligent supervision only existed because of another insured's intentional act (*i.e.*, sexual assault). Therefore, the claim fell outside the scope of coverage. *Id.* at 198.

10. Self-Insured Automobile Rental Companies

Automobile rental agreements will be considered stand-alone liability insurance contracts only if they include insurance provisions. Washington's Financial Responsibility Act (FLA) does not require self-insured rental car companies to provide third-party liability insurance to customers who reject optional liability insurance. *Shields v. Enterprise Leasing Company*, 139 Wash App 664, 161 P3d 1068 (2007).

B. PERSONAL INJURY PROTECTION (FIRST PARTY)

1. Coverage

> a. *Washington does not have mandatory PIP coverage. The law does require that the insured be offered PIP benefits as an "optional coverage." RCW 48.22.085; WAC 284-20-300.*
>
> b. *Rejection of the PIP benefit must be in writing by the named insured. If there is a valid rejection, then the rejection is binding on all levels of coverage and against all persons who might have been insured.*
>
> c. *If a rejection is made, subsequent renewals shall not have the PIP coverage included unless specifically requested, in writing, by the named insured.*

Various insurance policies have specific requirements written in the policy that available PIP insurance coverage is limited to those damages "arising out of a motor vehicle accident." *See, e.g., Tyrell v. Farmers Ins. Co.*, 140 Wash 2d 129, 994 P2d 833 (2000) (insured's injuries acquired from falling after stepping out of his mobile home were not caused by a "motor vehicle accident" as required in the policy. Thus, the insured was not entitled to PIP benefits); *see also Farmers Ins. Co. v. Grelis*, 43

Wash App 475, 478, 718 P2d 812 (1986) (court held the plain meaning of the "motor vehicle accident" evoked an image of one or more vehicles in forceful contact with another vehicle or person causing physical injury. Thus, an injury must result from an auto accident while the vehicle is being operated as an auto and an injury results from that operation).

2. Benefits

Several minimum and maximum PIP benefits exist and are limited to actual amount of loss or expense incurred.

    a. $10,000 (max $35,000) for medical and hospital benefits incurred within 3 years of the accident. RCW 48.22.095(1), RCW 48.22.100(1).

    b. $2,000 for funeral expenses. RCW 48.22.095(2), RCW 48.22.100(2).

    c. $10,000 (max $35,000) for one year income continuation benefits. This is limited to $200 (max $700) per week or 85% of the weekly income, whichever is less. RCW 48.22.095(3), RCW 48.22.100(3).

    d. $5,000 (max $14,600) for loss of services for one year after the accident, subject to $40 per day and $200 per week. The maximum coverage allows for $40 per day with no cap except it must be accrued within a year of the accident. RCW 48.22.095(4), RCW 48.22.100(4).

3. Other Insurance Clauses

    a.   PIP coverage of the vehicle will be primary over a passenger/driver's own PIP coverage.

    b.   In a pedestrian accident, the pedestrian may have other sources of coverage: his own policy under the policy of and that of the vehicle that hit him. Depending on the definition of "pedestrian", generally the vehicle is the primary insurance.

4. Basis for Denial – WAC 284-30-395

    a.   The insurer may only deny, limit or terminate benefits if the insurer determines the benefits are not reasonable, necessary, related to the accident or were not incurred within three years of the accident. WAC 284-30-395.

    b.   If the denial is based on the services not being reasonable, necessary or related to the accident, a health care professional must be consulted. These health care providers cannot be claim representatives, adjusters, managers or a care provider directly employed by the insurer. The health care provider consulted must be of the same health field or specialty as the insured's care provider. WAC 284-30-395(3)(a).

c. The insurer must provide a written explanation of the denial. This denial must describe the reasons for the action including copies of documents in support, if requested. The insurer must provide the reason given by the medical provider, in plain language, with whom the carrier consulted with to deny the claims. WAC 284-30-395(2).

d. A simple statement that the services are not reasonable and necessary is insufficient. WAC 284-30-395(2).

5. Disputes with an Insured

a. **Arbitration** – if there is an arbitration clause in the policy, the arbitration shall conform to the following:

   i. Shall take place within a reasonable time from the insured's request for arbitration.

   ii. Shall take place in the county where the insured resides.

   iii. Relaxed evidence rules apply and the rules will be similar to various named arbitration services.

b. **Bad Faith** – Washington requires all insurers to act in good faith in all insurance matters. RCW 48.01.030. *See* "Washington Bad Faith Claims," supra.

6. PIP Reimbursement

An insured is not required to reimburse an insurance company for PIP payments unless and until the insured has been fully compensated. This includes general damage for pain and suffering.

a. In *Thiringer v. American Motors Ins. Co.*, 91 Wash 2d 215, 588 P2d 191 (1978), the Washington Supreme Court held that: (1) where settlement exhausted the tortfeasor's assets, both present and prospective, the insurer, which had right of subrogation, was not prejudiced by such settlement, and (2) the insured was allowed to recoup general damages from the tortfeasor before allowing subrogation by the insurer for benefits payable under PIP coverage, as long as insured did not prejudice the rights of insurer.

b.	In other words, the insurer can recover only the excess which the insured has received from the wrongdoer after the insured has been fully compensated for his loss. *Id.* at 219. This principle is known as the "Thiringer Doctrine" and presents the question of whether a policy limits settlement has fully compensated the insured. Such a question may need to be determined by a finder of fact, such as arbitrator. *Roberts v. Safeco Ins. Co.*, 87 Wash App 604, 941 P2d 668 (1997).

c.	In cases where an insured is partially at fault for an accident and receives PIP benefits, the PIP insurer is not entitled to reimbursement for PIP payments until the insured has been fully compensated for his or her "total damages." In the context of PIP, Washington courts have held "total damages" to include all damages to which the insured is entitled before damages are reduced for the insured's own fault. *Sherry v. Financial Indemnity Co.*, 160 Wash 2d 611, 160 P3d 31 (2007).

d.	In *Loc Thien Truong v. Allstate Property & Casualty Ins.*, the Washington Court of Appeals held that settlement with the tortfeasor – for less than the tortfeasor's liability policy limits – was evidence of full compensation because the parties negotiated at "arms-length." Thus, a claimant cannot defeat the insurer's right to reimbursement with conclusory allegations that he settled for less than his actual damages. 151 Wash App 195, 211 P3d 430 (2009).

e.	In *State Farm Mutual Auto Ins. Co. v. Boyersmith,* the Court of Appeals held that when a policy provides an insurer the right to be reimbursed for PIP payments when the claimant is "fully compensated," courts may infer that full compensation has taken place without a trial on the issue. Claimants may rebut this inference, but such a rebuttal requires the presentation of some evidence. 149 Wash App 1035, --- P3d---- (2009) (*rev. denied State Farm Mutual Auto Ins. Co. v. Boyersmith,* 168 Wash 2d 1006, 226 P3d 781 (2010)) (This is an unpublished opinion. It cannot be cited as authority to a court of law.)

7.	**Attorney Fees on PIP Reimbursement**

The insured's attorney is likely entitled to attorney fees on PIP recoveries. Case law is developing as to the effect of different policy language. *See, e.g., Mahler v. Szucs*, 135 Wash 2d 398, 957 P2d 632 (1998); *Winters v. State Farm*, 144 Wash 2d 869, 31 P3d 1164 (2001).

a.   **Fully Insured Motorist**

In *Mahler v. Szucs*, 135 Wash 2d 398, 957 P2d 632 (1998), the Washington Supreme Court held that an insurer may be reimbursed for PIP payments made to an insured. Provided the insurer recognizes the public policy in Washington of full compensation of insureds and its other duties to insureds by statute, or common law, the insurer may establish its right to reimbursement and the mechanism for its enforcement by its contract with the insured. Thus, an insurer is required to share in the expenses (attorney fees and costs) incurred by the insured to recover the insurer's PIP payments from the tortfeasors. *Id.* at 436.

A common fund is created and the pro rate fee sharing rule is triggered by an injured party (a passenger or pedestrian) recovering under a tortfeasor's liability policy and a PIP policy issued by the same insurer. *Matsyuk v. State Farm Fire & Cas. Co.*, 173 Wash.2d 643, 272 P3d 802 (2012).

b.   **Underinsured Motorist**

     i.   In *Winters v. State Farm*, 99 Wash App 602, 994 P2d 881 (2000), the Washington Court of Appeals held that the insurer was entitled to reimburse itself for the PIP payments it had made. It also concluded that the insurer did not waive its rights to seek reimbursement by attempting to recover from the tortfeasor. However, the insurer was required to pay a pro rata share of the attorney fees and costs that the insured incurred in litigation.

     ii.   In *Safeco Ins. Co. v. Woodley*, 102 Wash App 384, 8 P3d 304 (2000), the court concluded that the insurance company could offset the settlement and PIP benefits, but had to pay a pro rata share of the legal expenses incurred to get those results. In other words, the insurance company had to pay a percentage of attorney fees equal to the amount it had paid in PIP benefits divided by the amount of the total damages.

c.   **Uninsured Motorists and PIP Benefits**

     i.   In *Hamm v. State Farm Mutual Auto. Ins. Co.*, 151 Wash 2d 303, 88 P3d 395 (2004), the insured was involved in an automobile accident with an uninsured motorist. The Washington Supreme Court held that the same pro rata sharing rule that applies in fully insured and underinsured motorist cases (*Mahler and Winters*) applies in uninsured motorist cases – *i.e.,* no matter how much insurance a tortfeasor has or does not have, an insurer must pay a pro rata share of the insured's legal fees in order to be reimbursed for PIP payments.

d. **Summary of the Fee Sharing Formula (*Mahler, Wint-ers, Hamm*):**

    i.   You need four numbers to determine the fee sharing amount:

         1)   The amount of the common fund of recoveries from all sources of liability insurance and UIM coverage ("CF" for "common fund");

         2)   The amount of the claimed reimbursement ("CR" for claimed reimbursement");

         3)   The actual amount of attorneys fees charged ("F" for actual attorneys fees); and

         4)   The actual amount of costs charged ("C" for actual costs).

Note: The costs have not been strictly limited to the statutory costs defined in RCW 4.84.

    ii.   The formula below will yield the final reimbursement amount ("FR" for "final reimbursement").

$$FR = CR - ((CR/CF) * (F + C))$$

Note: There are not three different formulas for Mahler, Winters, and Hamm. These are simply three different subsets of the same formula where the common fund of recoveries from liability and UIM consist of (1) all liability which is Mahler, (2) both liability and UIM which is Winters, and (3) all UM which is Hamm.

e. **Collision Coverage Payments**

    i.   In *Meas v. State Farm Fire and Cas. Co.*, 130 Wash App 527, 123 P3d 519 (2005), an insured argued that the same pro rata attorney fees sharing rule should apply to property damage payments under collision coverage. Plaintiff was involved in an accident for which she was not at fault. Plaintiff's insurer, State Farm, compensated her for her property damages, then sought reimbursement from the tortfeasor's insurer. After successfully recovering its property damage payment from the other insurer, State Farm reimbursed Plaintiff for her collision deductible. Plaintiff claimed that she should have been allowed to recover the property damages in her personal injury suit, which she argued would have made State Farm responsible for a pro rata share of her attorney fees. The court rejected this argument, however, holding that the property damage claim (and collision coverage) was separate from Plaintiff's personal injury claim, therefore, State Farm had a right under the policy to settle it directly with the other insurer at any time regardless of its insured's contrary desire.

Caution: Meas involved policies with separate limits for bodily injury and property damages. The same rationale may not apply to policies with combined limits.

C. UNINSURED/UNDERINSURED MOTORIST COVERAGE (FIRST PARTY)

Washington does not differentiate between UM and UIM; it is all under the same statutory scheme. An underinsured motor vehicle is defined as a vehicle with insufficient insurance to compensate the plaintiff's damages.

1. Coverage

Coverage must be offered, but like PIP, the insured is able to opt out of the coverage with a written rejection of the coverage. UIM property damage coverage can require a deductible up to $300 for hit and run, and $100 for all other accidents.

2. Coverage Provided When:

a. **There is Personal Injury, Death or Property Damage** as a result of an at-fault underinsured motorist (one who has no insurance or has limits insufficient to cover the damages).

b. **Phantom Vehicles** – A phantom vehicle is one which causes property damage to the insured property but which has no physical contact with it. The facts of the accident must be corroborated by competent evidence other than the testimony of the insured, or by any person with an underinsured motorist claim. The accident also must be reported to the authorities within 72 hours.

    i. An insured can use evidence of his or her own excited utterances to satisfy UIM statutory and policy requirements for corroboration of phantom vehicle by "competent evidence other than the testimony of the insured." *Nationwide Ins. v. Williams*, 71 Wash App 336, 858 P2d 516 (1993); *Gerken v. Mutual of Enumclaw Ins. Co.*, 74 Wash App 220, 872 P2d 1108 (1994).

c. **Hit and Run** – Questions have arisen as to what is the definition of a hit-and-run driver. In *State Farm v. Seaman*,

96 Wash App 629, 980 P2d 288 (1999), the court held that a hit-and-run vehicle is one whose driver flees the scene. A driver who stops after an accident, but does not exchange identification information with the other driver because they agree no damages or injuries have been sustained, is not a hit-and-run driver. *Id.* at 635.

    d.   **Good Samaritans** – Whether a person is "vehicle oriented" or actually touching a vehicle at the time of an accident is irrelevant to whether he is entitled to UM/UIM benefits. Thus, if a Good Samaritan stops his vehicle to assist a stranded motorist and is injured while providing assistance, he may be entitled to UM/UIM benefits from both his own insurance policy *and* the policy of the stranded motorist regardless of whether he was actually touching or inside either vehicle. *Butzberger v. Foster*, 151 Wash 2d 396, 89 P3d 689 (2004).

3.   Floating – Interaction with the Tortfeasor Policy

Washington requires the UIM policy float on top of the tortfeasor policy. In other words, if the tortfeasor has a minimum $25,000 policy, as does the insured, the total maximum coverage is $50,000. The UIM coverage floats on top of the settlement with the tortfeasor. Hamilton v. Farmers Ins. Co. of Washington, 107 Wash 2d 721, 733 P2d 213 (1987).

4.   No Exhaustion

Any provision in a UIM policy that requires the insured to exhaust the tortfeasor policy before pursuing the UIM benefit is invalid. However, a UIM carrier is entitled to a credit for the tortfeasor's liability limits if the insured chose to pursue UIM first.

5.   Limits of UIM

The carrier is required to offer the same limits as the liability policy. The insured can reduce the amount of UIM coverage in writing.

6.   Calculation of Benefits

    a.   In order to calculate UIM benefits, the total damage is first determined and then reduced by the amount of the insured's own fault. This leaves the recoverable amount from the tortfeasor. The tortfeasor's policy limits are then applied. Any additional amount of damages is the UIM benefit.

7. PIP Credit

The UIM carrier is allowed a credit, or offset, for PIP benefits it has paid, so long as the insured can be made whole. Hamm v. State Farm Mutual Auto. Ins. Co., 151 Wash 2d 303, 88 P3d 395 (2004). In other words, there is a credit if the insured's total damages can be satisfied within the tortfeasor's policy limit, and the UIM limit with a reduction for PIP. If the injury is too great, there will not be a credit for PIP paid.

However, the UIM carrier may not offset PIP benefits paid by other insurers. See Schlener v. Allstate Ins. Co., 121 Wash App 384, 88 P3d 993 (2004) (holding that provision in UIM policy that allowed insurer to offset PIP awards was void because it improperly reduced the amount of payable UIM benefits).

8. Subrogation/Consent to Settle

The insured must protect the subrogation rights of the insurer. The insurer has a subrogation interest in any amount it pays in UIM benefits to its insured to the extent that the tortfeasor's personal assets could satisfy the payment. Therefore, insurers regularly have consent to settle clauses, requiring the insured to obtain consent of the UIM carrier before settling with the tortfeasor. However, the insurer cannot unreasonably refuse to provide consent. The carrier, if it will not consent, essentially must pay the settlement amount to the insured, and carry out the action in the name of the insured.

The Washington Supreme Court addressed the effect of an insured settling for less than the tortfeasor's policy limits and a UIM claim in *Hamilton v. Farmers Ins. Co. of Washington*, 107 Wash 2d 721, 733 P2d 213 (1987). In *Hamilton*, the court held: (1) UIM coverage "floats" on top of the tortfeasor's liability limits, regardless of the amount of actual settlement; (2) any subrogation provisions in a UIM policy that would have the effect of diminishing the insured's full compensation are invalid; (3) the insurance company's statutory right of reimbursement is subject to *Thiringer* principles (permitting the insurer to be reimbursed ONLY from the insured's excess recovery); (4) the insurer may preserve its subrogation rights against the tortfeasor's assets by paying UIM benefits to the insured and paying the insured the full amount of his proposed settlement with the tortfeasor; and (5)the proceeds from any subrogation claim by the insurer against the tortfeasor must go first to providing full compensation to the insured, and only then toward reimbursement of the insurer.

9. Policy Exclusions

A policy exclusion of vehicles covered under the liability coverage from the definition of an underinsured motor vehicle may or may not be valid, depending on the identity of the claimant. Such exclusions are designed to prevent a passenger in an insured vehicle from asserting the negligence of the driver in order to secure recovery under the third-party coverage in addition to submitting a claim for UIM benefits as a first-party claimant.

a.   **Valid Exclusions** – Instances where these exclusions are valid include where omnibus insureds did not pay for the UIM protection for which they claim. In the absence of an exclusion, they would be entitled to UIM protection only because they happen to be in the covered vehicle at the time of the accident. Omnibus insureds had the ability to secure their own UIM coverage. Even if they failed to protect themselves by purchasing their own UIM coverage, they are still entitled to recovery under the liability coverage insuring the covered vehicle. *Blackburn v. Safeco Ins. Co.*, 115 Wash 2d 82, 794 P2d 1259 (1990).A UIM exclusion for a snowmobile is valid. *American States Ins. Co. v. Bolin*, 122 Wash App 717, 94 P3d 1010 (2004).

An example of a valid "owned vehicle" exclusion is when the insured was driving a vehicle owned by his live-in significant other, and the vehicle was not listed as a covered vehicle under the insured's policy. *Hann v. Progressive Northwestern Ins. Co.*, 162 Wash App 760 (2011) (*Note: this is an unpublished opinion and cannot be cited as authority, and is only demonstrative of how the court approaches the issues involved in this case*).

b.   **Invalid Exclusions** – Family member exclusions have been held to be invalid. In *Tissell v. Liberty Mutual Insurance Company*, 115 Wash 2d 107, 795 P2d 126 (1990), the Washington Supreme Court held that certain victim exclusions in UIM policies were invalid as a matter of public policy when asserted against the purchaser of a UIM policy. Such an exclusion is invalid where the claimant is a named insured or family member of a named insured. The named insured has paid for UIM coverage for her and family, designed to provide a second tier of coverage above whatever liability coverage possessed by the negligent driver. Thus, a family member exclusion of a UIM policy is void.

10.   Disputes with an Insured

Virtually all policies require arbitration.

a.   **Arbitration**

i.   **Issues of Liability and/or Damages are Proper for Arbitration**. Nearly all UIM policies provide for arbitration of UIM claims. However, inclusion of such a provision for arbitration is not mandatory, and the insurer is free to omit it from its policy. *Price v. Farmers Ins. Co.*, 133 Wash 2d 490, 946 P2d 388 (1997).

ii.   **Concurrent Claims Against the Tortfeasor and UIM Carrier.** If the UIM insurer has notice of the lawsuit against the tortfeasor, the insurer will be bound by the court's findings as to liability and damages under a doctrine similar to res judicata or collateral estoppels. To protect itself, the insurer must either move to intervene in the tort action, or demand early arbitration pursuant to the policy. *Fisher v. Allstate Ins. Co.*, 136 Wash 2d 240, 251, 961 P2d 350 (1998).The question of how much notice must be given to the insurer of an impending trial in order for them to be bound by the results was addressed in *Lenzi v. Redland Ins. Co.*, 140 Wash 2d 267, 996 P2d 603 (2000). The court held for the insured, stating the insurer had received sufficient notice (copy of summons and complaint) to put a reasonable party on notice that a lawsuit was underway that could affect its own interests. *Id.* at 276.

iii.   **Scope of Arbitration.** Nothing in the Washington Mandatory Arbitration Rules precludes an arbitrator from determining all issues raised by the pleadings, including off-set/set-off issues in a suit for UIM benefits. If an arbitrator decides to place these issues outside the scope of arbitration, a trial court may permissibly reduce a mandatory arbitration award by PIP and liability payments. *Mercier v. Geico*, 139 Wash App 891, 165 P3d 375 (2007) (*abrogated on other grounds by Little v. King,* 147 Wash App 883, 198 P3d 525 (2008)).

iv.   Washington courts believe that if there is a coverage dispute, the proper forum is court. Therefore, if the insurer denies coverage, the insured must seek relief through a declaratory action or a motion to compel arbitration.

In *Price v. Farmers Ins. Co.*, 133 Wash 2d 490, 946 P2d 388 (1997), the Washington Court of Appeals held that the arbitration award represented the insured's total damages and the insurer was entitled to offset its UIM payment with PIP payments made. Upon review, the Supreme Court reversed, holding that UIM arbitration clauses are limited to determination of tortfeasor liability and calculation of total damages. The jurisdiction of the trial and appellate courts are limited to resolve only those issues presented to the arbitrators. Any finding on a question that was not submitted to the arbitrators is outside the jurisdiction of the trial or appellate courts. *Id.* Therefore, any remaining issue as to PIP offset coverage must be resolved by agreement or a separate action under the general jurisdiction of the superior court. *Id.* at 502.

In *Heaphy v. State Farm Mutual Auto Ins. Co.*, 117 Wash App 438, 72 P3d 220 (2003), the court held that the question of whether the plaintiff had suffered diminished value damages was not a question of coverage, and thus arbitration was appropriate.

v. **Time** – the policy may require that the arbitration demand must be made within a reasonable time of the dispute. The lack of a time period in the policy can lead to an endless limitation period.

vi. ***Attorney Fees** – The general rule is that an attorney fee award is required any time the insurer compels the insured to assume the burden of legal action in order to obtain the full benefit of his or her insurance contract, regardless of whether the insurer's duty to defend is at issue. However, no attorney fees are awarded to an insured in arbitrating a UIM coverage claim, taking legal action to determine the liability of a tortfeasor, or determining the extent of the insured's damages. Olympic Steamship Co. v. Centennial Ins. Co., 117 Wash 2d 37, 811 P2d 673 (1991).*

vii. In *Olympic*, the Court recognized the disparity of bargaining power between an insurance company and its policyholder. When an insured purchases an insurance contract he seeks protection from expenses arising from litigation, not vexing, expensive litigation with its insurer. *Id.* at 52. However, "Olympic Steamship" attorney fees cannot be recovered if the insured breaches policy conditions and the breach potentially relieved the insurer of the obligation to provide coverage. *Public Util. Dist. No. 1 of Klickitat County v. International Ins. Co.*, 124 Wash 2d 789, 881 P2d 1020 (1994).

viii. **Bad Faith** – Washington requires all insurers to act in good faith in all insurance matters. RCW 48.01.030. *See* "Washington Bad Faith Claims," supra.

APPENDIX 1

PROPOSED FORM LETTERS – ADVANCE PAYMENT

[DATE]

Mr. Joe Smith
123 S.W. Main Street
Wherever, USA 12345

Re: Our Insured   :   _____
       Claim Number   :   _____
       Date of Accident   :   _____
       Location of Accident   :   _____

Dear Mr. Smith:

      ABC Insurance Company recently made an "advance payment" toward either your property damage claim or medical bills as part of the claim you have made as a result of the above accident. Because ABC Insurance Company has made an advance payment, we are required by ORS 12.155 to tell you that there is a time limitation for any claim for damages. The period of limitation for commencement of an action for damages as set by Chapter 12 of the Oregon Revised Statutes will expire on _____.

      ABC Insurance Company has extended these benefits during the claim process as a courtesy to you. However, if you obtain any judgment in your favor in the future, ABC Insurance Company intends to apply the amount of the advance payment as a credit.

      Thank you for your attention to this matter.

                        Very truly yours,

                        Claims Representative

APPENDIX 2

PROPOSED FORM LETTER - PIP CLAIMS

[DATE]

Mr. Joe Smith
123 S.W. Main Street
Wherever, USA 12345

Re: Our Insured   :   _____
          Claim Number   :   _____
          Date of Accident :   _____
          Location of Accident :   _____

Dear Mr. Smith:

       This letter is to formally notify you that ABC Insurance Company accepts coverage of your claim for Personal Injury Protection benefits due pertaining to the above-referenced loss.

       If a dispute were to arise between us with regard to the amount of benefits due, we agree to submit the dispute to binding arbitration restricted to that issue only.

                                 Very truly yours,

                                 Claims Representative

APPENDIX 3

PROPOSED FORM LETTER – UIM CLAIMS

[DATE]

Mr. Joe Smith
123 S.W. Main Street
Wherever, USA 12345

Re: Our Insured   :   _____
     Claim Number   :   _____
     Date of Accident   :   _____
     Location of Accident   :   _____

Dear Mr. Smith:

      This letter is to formally notify you that ABC Insurance Company accepts coverage of your claim for Underinsured Motorist benefits pertaining to the above-referenced loss.

      If a dispute were to arise between us with regard to liability and/or the amount of damages, we agree to submit the dispute to binding arbitration restricted to those issues only.

                    Very truly yours,

                    Claims Representative

APPENDIX 4

PROPOSED FORM LETTER – UM CLAIMS

[DATE]

Mr. Joe Smith
123 S.W. Main Street
Wherever, USA 12345

Re: Our Insured   :   _____
       Claim Number   :   _____
       Date of Accident   :   _____
       Location of Accident   :   _____

Dear Mr. Smith:

       This letter is to formally notify you that ABC Insurance Company accepts coverage of your claim for Uninsured Motorist benefits pertaining to the above-referenced loss.

       If a dispute were to arise between us with regard to liability and/or the amount of damages, we agree to submit the dispute to binding arbitration restricted to those issues only.

                              Very truly yours,

                              Claims Representative

TABLE OF AUTHORITIES

CASES

TABLE OF AUTHORITIES

STATUTES

NOTES

Jeffrey W. Hansen
Partner

Contact
jhansen@smithfreed.com
111 SW 5th Ave, Ste 4300
Portland, OR 97204
503-227-2424-Phone
503-227-2535-Fax

Practice Areas
Automotive Defense
Business Litigation
Commercial Liability
Employment Litigation

Education
Drake University School of Law
and Center for Dispute Resolution,
J.D., *Order of the Coif*, 1992

University of Portland, B.S.,
Finance, 1988

Bar Admissions
Oregon

Professional Certification & Accolades
Member, Oregon State Bar Association

Member, Defense Research Institute

Member, American Bar Association,
Torts and Insurance Practice Section

Admitted, United States District Court
for the District of Oregon

American Board of Trial Advocates

Member, Litigation Counsel of America

Member, Oregon Association of
Defense Counsel (OADC)

Member, PHRMA

Chairman, Automobile Practice Group,
OADC, 2007-2008

Vice-Chairman, Automobile Practice
Group, OADC, 2006-2007

Publication Liaison, OADC, 2005-2006

Best Lawyers in America

Oregon Super Lawyers

PRACTICE FOCUS
Jeff's practice focuses on civil litigation in the state and federal courts of Oregon, with an emphasis in the defense of injury claims ranging from auto accidents to toxic exposures and products liability. Jeff's practice includes the defense of employment litigation, RICO, fraud and other commercial claims. Jeff is the firm's most active trial attorney, averaging eight jury trials per year.

SIGNIFICANT REPRESENTATION
Jeff has conducted over 100 jury trials and 270 arbitrations. He successfully defended homeowners in a case involving the wrongful death of a 6-year-old boy at their home. The boy's death was the result of near decapitation when a dumbwaiter he was inspecting was inadvertently activated, trapping him in the dumbwaiter shaft. After the parents filed suit, the young man's wrongful death case was settled for $520,000, of which our client, the homeowners, paid only $20,000. Jeff also successfully defended a woman in a wrongful death case brought by her ex-husband following the death of their 3-year-old child. This case was settled at a mediation following discovery and was resolved within an extraordinarily favorable outcome for the insurance carrier. Jeff successfully defended a married couple from Southwest Washington who caused a catastrophic car accident at the Portland International Airport. The accident resulted in the near amputation of the Plaintiff's legs, a 38-year-old oral surgeon with a thriving practice. Despite the fact that the medical expenses were $2.3 million and the estimated future wage loss exceeded $5 million, the case was settled well below the pre-filing demand and with minimal contribution from the clients. Jeff successfully defended an industrial turbine manufacturer in numerous lawsuits for personal injuries and wrongful deaths resulting from exposure to asbestos-containing materials used in the manufacture and maintenance of its products. To date, all of the cases have either been voluntarily dismissed, subject to summary judgment or resulted in judgments in favor of the Defendant at trial.

Jeff participated in the defense of Dow Chemical in the Oregon Breast Implant litigation as well as Showa Denko KK in the Oregon l-tryptophan litigation. Participated in the defense of Owens Corning Fiberglass in over 750 cases arising out of alleged exposure to Owens Corning products in tire factories in Central Iowa. Jeff successfully defended a recovering heroin addict in a multimillion-dollar personal injury suit (including punitive damages for intoxication) arising from a high-speed motor vehicle accident. Following a five-day jury trial, the plaintiff was awarded only $33,000. Jeff also successfully defended a regional pharmacy in a wrongful death suit for misprescribing narcotic medications, resulting in plaintiff's death. The pharmacy was granted summary judgment following discovery.

PUBLICATIONS AND PRESENTATIONS
Jeff has authored several articles related to Oregon insurance law and he regularly speaks to trade organizations and insurance companies regarding legislative changes affecting Oregon.

SF&E
SMITH FREED & EBERHARD P.C.
Your Litigation Partner

Joshua P. Hayward
Partner

Contact

jhayward@smithfreed.com
111 SW 5th Ave, Ste 4300
Portland, OR 97204
503-227-2424-Phone
503-227-2535-Fax

Practice Areas

Injury Defense
Wrongful Death Defense
Automotive Liability
Products Liability
Premises Liability

Education

Pepperdine University, J.D., 2001
Oregon State University, B.A., History, 1997

Bar Admissions

Oregon
Washington
California

Professional Certification & Accolades

Member, Oregon State Bar Association
Member, Washington State Bar Association
Member, California Bar Association
Member, Oregon Association of Defense Counsel
Member, Multnomah County Bar Association
Oregon Super Lawyers Rising Star

PRACTICE FOCUS

Josh's practice focuses on the defense of cases involving personal injury and wrongful death. He represents companies and the insureds of several large insurance carriers against claims arising from the alleged negligent use of motor vehicles, products liability and premises liability.

PROFESSIONAL BACKGROUND

Josh started as an associate at Smith Freed in 2001. He has been a partner since 2008. Josh leads a group of attorneys that specialize in trying cases and effective pre-trial litigation. Josh typically tries several cases a year to jury verdict.

Prior to joining Smith Freed & Eberhard, Josh gained experience in civil litigation, criminal defense, and family law clerking at a firm in Salem, Oregon. While attending law school, he spent time in London, UK, where he served as a Solicitor's clerk for a high profile firm advocating on behalf of individuals alleging human rights violations.

SIGNIFICANT REPRESENTATION

•Represents three of the top five largest personal lines auto insurers and their insureds in Oregon and Washington.

•Significant practice defending premises liability claims against property owners including churches, restaurants, stores, hotels, and bars.

•Has successfully litigated product liability claims involving national tire manufacturers, do it yourself home supply chains, equipment rental companies and engineering companies.

•Represents several local and regional commercial and personal lines insurers and their insureds in Oregon and Washington.

PUBLICATION AND PRESENTATIONS

Josh regularly gives presentations to claims professionals on legislative updates regarding Oregon and Washington insurance law.

SMITH FREED & EBERHARD P.C.
Your Litigation Partner

Kyle D. Riley
Partner

Contact

kriley@smithfreed.com
705 2nd Ave, 17th Floor
Seattle, WA 98104
206-576-7575-Phone
206-576-7580-Fax

Practice Areas

Automotive Defense
Commercial Liability Defense
Rental Vehicle Law
Bad Faith

Education

Northwestern School of Law of Lewis and Clark College, J.D.; *cum laude*, 2002
Pacific University, B.A. Mathematics & Political Science, 1998

Bar Admissions

Oregon
Washington

Professional Certification & Accolades

Member, Oregon State Bar Association
Member, Washington State Bar Association
Member, Oregon Association of Defense Counsel
Member, Washington Defense Trial Lawyers
Member, Oregon Casualty Adjusters Association
Member, Toastmasters International
Black Belt Trial Advocacy Training Program
Oregon Super Lawyer Rising Star 2009, 2010, 2011

PRACTICE FOCUS

Kyle Riley is a Partner at Smith Freed and Eberhard who helped launch the opening of the Seattle office. Prior to moving to Seattle, Kyle spent most of his time defending clients in the Puget Sound area. He specializes in defending personal injury claims and defending insurers who face bad faith allegations. Kyle has also defended clients in fire losses, trucking companies, banking institutions, and self-insured rental car companies.

PROFESSIONAL BACKGROUND

Prior to joining Smith Freed & Eberhard, Kyle worked with the Oregon Department of Justice where he gained significant litigation experience specializing in the recovery of self-insured losses. He joined Smith Freed & Eberhard in 2003.

SIGNIFICANT REPRESENTATION

Kyle has defended numerous personal injury claims and insurers who are alleged to have engaged in bad faith.

In *Bauducco-Heiss v. Jim Fruitt Trucking,* Kyle was the lead attorney who defended a truck driver and trucking company who were defendants in a lawsuit a very serious motor vehicle accident involving the death of two adults and a serious brain injury to a young girl. The case was extremely complicated due to claims being alleged against the State of Washington involving low tension cable barriers and a construction company. The liability limits were insufficient to compensate the plaintiffs. At mediation, the case was unable to settle due to coverage issues involving the codefendants. Kyle was able to locate a favorable witness and retain an expert to defeat the codefendant's attempts to be dismissed from the underlying case. The case ended in a global settlement.

In *Naylor v. Gwin & Sons Logging,* Kyle was the trial attorney for a logging company that was a third party defendant alleged to have cause damage to a pipeline or water system through their logging activities. The claim included a contractual right to attorney fees. Prior to trial Kyle negotiated a settlement with the third party plaintiff whereby all defendants would waive their rights to attorney fees from each other. The defense retained joint experts who were able to plot the pipeline, locate the source of some of the failures, and identified the located failures as being caused by freezing damage unrelated to the logging activities. During Kyle's cross-examination of the plaintiff's expert, the plaintiff's expert admitted that he did not measure the length of the line and assumed the line was as long as the plaintiff told him, which had been exaggerated. The jury returned a defense verdict after an hour of deliberation entitling the lead defendant to recover their attorney fees from the plaintiff.

SF&E SMITH FREED & EBERHARD P.C.
Your Litigation Partner

Katie D. Buxman
Partner

Contact

kbuxman@smithfreed.com
111 SW 5th Ave, Ste 4300
Portland, OR 97204
503-227-2424-Phone
503-227-2535-Fax

Practice Areas

Automobile Defense
Commercial Liability Defense
Special Investigation Unit
Coverage

Education

Gonzaga University School of Law,
J.D., 2002

Gonzaga University, B.A.
Psychology & Political Science, 1999

Bar Admissions

Oregon
Washington

Professional Certification & Accolades

Member, Oregon State Bar Association

Member, Washington State Bar
Association

Admitted, United States District Court,
Western District of Washington

Admitted, United States District Court,
Eastern District of Washington

Admitted, United States District Court,
District of Oregon

Admitted, Ninth Circuit Court of
Appeals

Oregon Super Lawyers Rising Star

PRACTICE FOCUS

Katie's practice specializes in representing insurance carriers and their insureds in personal injury, coverage and special investigation unit claims (SIU) in both Oregon and Washington. In addition, Katie has considerable experience handling insurance coverage and bad faith litigation.

PROFESSIONAL BACKGROUND

Prior to joining Smith Freed & Eberhard, Katie was a partner at an insurance defense firm in Vancouver, Washington where she gained significant experience defending casualty, insurance coverage, bad faith and appellate cases for multiple insurance carriers. She evaluated all aspects of first and third party insurance claims, represented several cases at trial and successfully argued Motions before both Oregon and Washington courts.

SIGNIFICANT REPRESENTATION

Katie's significant experience includes representing an operator of a boat whereby the passenger suffered a traumatic leg amputation. The case settled successfully out of court. She also represented an operator of a boat whereby the individual being towed behind the boat suffered a brain injury. The case settled below policy limits. She received a defense verdict on an auto liability case in Multnomah County Circuit Court. In 2011, she obtained a complete defense verdict in Multnomah County in a suspected minor impact fraud case involving four Plaintiffs where the Plaintiffs were seeking almost $500,000 in damages. She also received a favorable verdict at trial in Klamath Falls Circuit Court on an auto liability case whereby the Plaintiff was seeking several thousand dollars but the jury only awarded a nominal amount.

PUBLICATION AND PRESENTATIONS

Katie enjoys speaking to trade organizations and insurance companies regarding Oregon and Washington law. Some of the groups she has presented to include: Oregon Casualty Adjusters Association, International Association of SIU Investigators and the Oregon Association of Defense Counsel.

SMITH FREED & EBERHARD P.C.
Your Litigation Partner